21st Centur
(and husband)

Or rather… the trials and tribulations of being a modern day father and husband (also told from the perspective of his wife)

By 21st Century Dad

Dedicated to my wonderful (no, really) family!

Table of Contents

Introduction

The husband's entry

You know when you settle down to watch a good movie and just after the opening credits have finished rolling the words *'Based on a true story'* flash up on the screen?

Well that's the point at which my wife always, and without fail, makes a big point of nudging me in the ribs causing me to spill my popcorn everywhere as she once again informs me....

"Oo, oo... look, based on a true story!"

Thanks honey!

Now I clearly understand what that film maker meant when he added in that superimposition, because up until you pointed that out for me I didn't have a bloody clue what that could possibly mean.

My wife and I rarely watch films together.

It's true.

My wife and I always *sit down* to watch a film together....

However within ten minutes of the movie opening she's there, head back, mouth wide open, snoring away.

I've gotten so used to it over the years that I just don't notice now.

It's like living close to a major airport and inviting friends down from the countryside to stay and they can't sleep due to all the noise and you think it's weird because you don't even notice it anymore.

It's like that.

We went to the cinema with a load of friends once to see the very first *'Lord of the Rings'* movie.

There was so many of us we took up the first few rows of the auditorium.

Ten, maybe fifteen minutes into the movie, one of my friends, sitting in front of me, turned round and said....

"Wake your missus up mate, I can't hear the bloody film!"

Sure enough she was catching flies and doing her best impression of a tractor starting up.

And then once the 'Based on a true story' film is finished, we have the same old conversation on the way home that basically involves me explaining that 'yes I do think it was based on a true story, but as it was so unbelievable, Hollywood has clearly gotten hold of it, completely removed any of the original facts or references to the actual story and instead introduced their typical movie template where a good looking protagonist battles against a stereotypical antagonist, loses, meets a beautiful women, gets himself back on his feet as a result, has another battle with the antagonist and possible even a car chase and consequently defeats the antagonist, falls in love with the beautiful woman and everyone's happy -- AGAIN!... it's as far removed from the original story as you can possible get'.

You may have to read that last bit again!

If I ever do want the conscious company of another living person to share in my movie experience, I simply tell my wife 'hey honey, this is based on a true story' and she'll do her utmost to stay awake.

For all of ten minutes.

"Are you sure 'Lesbian, Vampire, Zombie Killers' is based on a true story?"

"Yes my sweet -- now pass the Revels!"

It's like she has an 'off' switch.

If only ☺

It's the same when we head off to bed.

I generally finish in the bathroom first as I have (a LOT) less to do, and plus being the male of the household I have to set the alarm clock (if it were left to her, the first time we'd be aware that it was morning would be when the school phoned to see where the kids were) and ensure the TV in the bedroom still works -- which she hates.

"Do you have to watch that thing every night?"

"Yes my little flower... it drowns out your snoring!"

Plus, once I'm in bed I can be laying there for anything up to twenty minutes while the blow torch gets hot enough for her to burn her make-up off with.

Then she has to apply all those incredibly expensive creams she always gets conned in to buying.

Anti-wrinkle this and anti-wrinkle that.

Do women really believe that slapping some expensive cream on at night is really going to stop them from getting older?

'The more expensive it is, the better it has to be!'

Oh no my little sugar plum fairy... the more expensive it is, the dafter YOU have to be!

I'm going to go into business selling re-branded, overpriced, whipped cream as an anti-aging cure and make a fortune.

Then she has to floss, which oh my God, I really don't need to be in the bathroom to share in that experience.

And, by the way, she only flosses now because of peer pressure (as you will read about later).

Then brush her teeth with the electric toothbrush.

Then apply more whipped cream that does something else.

Then a total body lotion.

It's a surprise she doesn't jump into bed and slide straight out the other side.

And then she'll insist on a kiss goodnight.

Now I don't know how many other men have to endure a similar nightly ritual that ends in a goodnight kiss, but after she's caked herself in all that grease, it would be less slimy kissing a slug.

And so by the time her *'nightly care routine'* is complete -- and don't forget she also has to lay her clothes out ready for the school mum's designer clothes parade at the school gates the next day and it takes about twenty minutes for her to mix and match and find something that no one will have seen her in before that is also made by some bloke with an Italian sounding name... it's time to get up!

So, I give her the customary final *'What?! Are you serious? Just in case one of us really doesn't wake up in the morning, are you expecting to get murdered in your sleep then?'* -- kiss, and before I even get to lean over and switch off my bedside light she's fast asleep.

That's how bad it is.

I think she has Narcolepsy as she starts doing nodding dog impressions if she simply stands still for too long.

I'm sure she could sleep standing up -- like a horse.

And so it is with this book.

'Based on a true story'.

And one you'll be pleased to know that Hollywood hasn't gotten hold of.

At least not yet anyway!

And if Hollywood *is* reading this... then as long as Brad Pitt plays me and the money's right... you can do what you want with it for all I care.

Which I think is generally what the owner of the rights to the *'original story'* they've just ruined must have said judging by how much they spoiled it.

And so, to recap -- just in case you missed the whole point of this introduction....

Ninety percent of what you read in this book actually happened.

It's true.

Ninety percent ACTUALLY happened!

Even as it was being written and friends were proof reading it for us they were constantly asking....

"Did that REALLY happen?"

Yes!

It REALLY did!

Ninety percent of it anyway.

That's how *'interesting'* (I think) our life is.

The other ten percent....

Well... Hollywood *may* have just gotten hold of it a little.

But only a little.

And at least for now anyway!

And that ten percent is not there to protect the innocent....

Or to 'Hollywood up' the stories somewhat.

No.

It's there to stop anyone that I may have casually mentioned in one of the chapters from recognising themselves.

Or even me.

And suing me.

And perhaps now and again to make it a little more interesting to read.

Maybe even get a little point or two across.

Or maybe just to (*hopefully*) make you smile a little.

So I really do, genuinely, hope that you not only enjoy this book, but that you also get something out of reading about....

'The trials and tribulations of bringing up kids, keeping a (very) (only joking) (not really) demanding wife happy, and all the while trying desperately to earn a bit of a living.

Written by a 21st Century Dad....

And his wife!

Chapter One

Fun Days Out

The husband's entry

It was 6.51am.

Summer time.

And I had had an epiphany!

I lay there, staring up at the ceiling, mulling it over in my head as the first new light of dawn gently crept in through the curtains, warmly illuminating the bedroom when THUD, my wife's elbow hit me square in the forehead.

It wasn't the first time either.

Oh no… it seems that this misguided elbow trajectory thing is becoming a bit too much of a regular occurrence just lately as she rolls over to *'snuggle.'*

'Snuggle.'

It's an interesting word that roughly translates into *'let's not actually get out of bed for another ten minutes.'*

I wouldn't mind but it takes her an hour to get ready.

What the hell has she got to do?

It's not like she resembles some extra in a *'Night of the Living Dead'* movie first thing in the morning.

Me, I just jump out of bed, pull on the same clothes that lay where I kicked them off the night before and after a quick toilet stop I'm downstairs, radio on and making two rounds of toasted, peanut butter covered fruity bagels topped with a slivering of sliced banana, all washed down with a glass of ice cold milk for the offspring.

Then it's another quick stop off at the cat's bedroom (utility room) and before the kettle has even flicked itself off, there's Felix in their two bowls and the school shoes are polished.

And so it was today, just like every other school day.

"Boris needs crickets."

I spin round to see my son shuffling over to the breakfast bar in nothing more than his Ben 10 slippers and oversized pants.

His latest copy of Robert Muchamore clutched tightly in his hand.

Morning reading.

My son's a bookworm.

His idea of heaven is playing Minecraft on the Ipad, but as we like to adopt more of an '*old fashioned*' approach to parenting we tend to limit the time he actually gets to play Minecraft on the Ipad to... well, very little.

I'm not against all this new technology.

Please don't think that for one minute.

In fact I do actually embrace it.

I'm writing this now on a PC, so there you go.

We visited the Roald Dahl museum with the kids one school half term and I was astounded to discover that he wrote all his books using just a pencil and paper.

What was I expecting really?

Especially if you consider the fact that Microsoft Word was still just a twinkle in Bill Gate's eye when old Roald was writing.

Just goes to show how much we now take the home PC for granted.

Almost as much as spell check.

And the calculator.

I still don't see why schools insist on teaching kids how to work out all those maths sums when *everything* has a calculator either in it, or on it, in this day and age.

It literally takes me less time to switch on my phone, open the calculator app and punch in the numbers than it does to hunt around for some scrap paper, then try to find a pencil (and an eraser -- force of habit!) and then try to find somewhere or something to lean on because *you* try writing on a piece of used tissue with a sharp pencil while standing up.

Our kids come home every week with spellings to learn over the weekend for their big test on Monday morning.

And it's nothing but, stress, stress, stress.

Not for them though.

For the wife... who can't bear to think of either of our offspring getting less than FULL marks on their spelling because how could she then face the other mums down at the school pick-up fashion parade when the first thing those mums ask their kids is not '*how was your day?*' but '*what was your score?*'

Why do you need to know how to spell when spell check does all that for you?

It's like, why bother to push a vacuum cleaner back and forth over our dirty carpets when they've now invented 'Roomba?!'

Not the greatest example I grant you.

But seriously... who's going to write anything on paper, with a pencil (and an Oxford English dictionary next to them) in this day and age now anyway?

And what was the deal with an Oxford English Dictionary anyway?

They were there to help you spell a word correctly but you still needed to know how to spell the word correctly in order to be able to look up how to spell it correctly.

And what makes the people of Oxford so good at spelling?

But the Roald Dahl museum was one of those desperate attempts to actually do something other than the usual same old, same old, half term activities that basically go like:

Visit a THEME PARK.
My wife always thinks that if we go at the beginning of the week it will be quiet as most people will wait till nearer the end of the week.

It never is.

So we spend the same amount of money on this as we would do on say... going to the theatre, only to spend most of the day moaning about how expensive everything is because they have a captive audience and about how long the bloody queues are.

I never really seemed to notice the queues when I was a teenager.

Funny that.

"Let's get some fast track tickets dad. They're only ninety seven pounds each for unlimited access to all the rides".

It's true they were.

Ninety seven pounds each!

What a bargain.

Especially after I've already paid the same amount as I would to purchase a small family car to get in in the first place.

Do people actually spend ninety seven pounds EACH, on unlimited fast track tickets?

I guess they must do.

What was the conversation like in the marketing meeting that came up with that one?

"You know what... people are pretty stupid really. Not only can we ramp up our entrance fees yet again this year, over charge for the crap we serve called food but let's see, for a laugh, if we can actually get someone to spend ninety seven pounds each on unlimited fast track tickets."

I bought four of them.

And then spent the day doing... guess what?

That's right.

Bloody queuing!

Because EVERYONE else had also bought fast track tickets.

So a total of eight hours and two rides later and next week we're off to....

The THEATRE.
"FOUR HUNDRED POUNDS! To watch people dance around on a stage. Are you kidding me?!"

I admit my reply probably wasn't the best.

Being a former dancer my wife has grown up around all those luvvies and in turn has tried her best to educate me in the wonders of the theatre.

I say educate.

What I actually mean is… dragged me, kicking and screaming to pretty much all the West End shows over the years.

And just when I thought there were no more to see.

That it was all over.

I'd served my time.

I can be awarded that 'HUSBAND OF THE DECADE' award….

My daughter is born.

So now I'm seeing them all over again.

And I wouldn't mind but really… FOUR HUNDRED POUNDS!

Apparently you *can* get cheaper seats but that would be no good, because you wouldn't actually be able to see anything because there'll be a bloody great pillar in the way.

So then we go ….

BOWLING.
I'm so bored of bowling.

We always go with another family and their dad is SO much better at bowling than me.

If it wasn't for the fact that my kids would disown me, I'd actually have those little rail things up.

Even my eight year old daughter doesn't have those up any more.

"It's just not *'street'* dad."

And every time, their dad makes a big thing about *'taking it easy on me this time'* and *'giving me a chance'* and then proceeds to humiliate me in front of my wife and kids.

I think in the cavemen times the alpha male didn't just fight it out with the other male and steal his mate.

No!

They played them at ten pin bloody bowling and did it that way instead.

You know what's worse than bowling?

A BIKE RIDE!

We're quite fortunate to have a great big park quite close to us which we often bike round much to the frustration of all the speed walkers (what's that all about by the way? They just look like they've tripped and are desperately trying to catch their balance before they face plant, teeth first into the concrete) and couples, young and old, hoping for a nice leisurely stroll around the great, four mile lake (everything's 'great' in the 'great park').

How wrong they are!

Because if you don't get jogged to death, you'll get run down by all the families with the same idea as us, desperately trying to do something with the kids on the cheap which inevitably ends up with us all in the overpriced coffee shop while my wife intravenously injects coffee into her bloodstream and the kids load up on sugar and carbs completely undoing all of the good work we've just done.

But the thrill of the bike ride is somewhat let down when you actually have to drive there.

Surely the whole point is the actual riding bit, but oh no, I have to spend longer attaching the bike rack to the back of the car, loading all the bikes on, strapping them up tight, then taking them off again as I've inevitably forgotten to unload the boot and we can't access the picnic blanket and Frisbee with the bike rack on it.

Then, checking and re-checking that everything's secure and one's not going to slide off and bring the A322 to a stand still... again, by which time it would have actually been quicker to have biked there.

On top of that my wife doesn't actually enjoy riding a bike.

Me, I like to get the heart rate up a bit, blood pumping, y'know.

Whereas my wife is more the... *'Driving Miss Daisy... but on a bike'* type of cyclist.

Before kids we'd bike quite a bit.

I think she was still trying to convince me she was an *'active'* kind of girl.

Up for anything that I was up for.

But it was short lived and I ended up buying her an old second hand electric bike off Ebay which was great for a short while until someone nicked the battery when it was parked up in the bike rack at Centreparcs.

So that was the end of that.

We had to get rid of the bike in the end because it was actually so heavy she might as well have tried pedalling a tractor for all the huffing and puffing she was doing.

And what was someone going to do with the battery anyway?

It took at least three power lifters to be able to get the thing off the ground although I guess if you were somehow able to wire it up to the mains it might power your house for all of... oh, sixty seconds, because that's all it managed to last for when it was powering her bike.

Where was I?

Oh yes, so when I was a kid I used to actually go outside and play... with other kids.

I'd walk three miles, knock on a friends door, only to be told by his mum that he was already down the park playing.

I never considered it to be that big a deal really.

The other day our next door neighbour phoned to ask if we had a parcel of theirs as they'd been out all day and the van driver had stuck a card through their door saying we had it.

I was almost expecting them to ask me to drop it round as well.

And if the van driver had stuck a card through their door saying that we had it, why did she need to phone?

And besides that… WHY did she phone?

See, I object to all this technology when it makes us even lazier.

So as time on the Ipad is limited to *"what does your mother think?"* his second idea of heaven is to simply curl up in a corner and read a book.

His reading is actually quite advanced for his age.

One of the teenagers at one of his many after school clubs lent him a book aimed at the slightly older reader.

We were a bit concerned with the content but as it contained some big words that would make it hard to read we didn't think he'd enjoy it and would soon put it down.

He read it in a day.

And then the next one.

And the next one.

In the end he read the whole series and moved on to the second series.

And then the third.

In record time.

And then we got the phone call.

"I'm a bit concerned about the story your son's written in his creative writing class" said his teacher.

Apparently the school thought the story *was* very creative however it was the content of the story that they were most concerned about.

It went something like this.

And I summarise.

The protagonist in the story... my son, needed to make some money to buy himself his own Ipad as he wasn't allowed to spend much time on the family one.

So, as his parents were both druggies, he stole some of their cocaine, snook out of the house late at night, walked into town and sold it on the streets, thus making himself a small fortune with which he then used to buy himself an Ipad at one of those *'exchange your unwanted goods for cash'* kind of places.

It's true!

Now I'll be honest... I do like the odd bottle of Kopparberg at a weekend but that hardly qualifies me for the lead in the next Trainspotting movie.

So needless to say we're now under close scrutiny by his school and he's back to reading 'Noddy and Big Ears' books.

Chapter Two

Snuggle Time

The wife's entry

6.30am and I was wide awake although my eyes were still closed as I desperately fought to get back to sleep again... but it just wasn't happening.

It's the height of summer and we had sunlight streaming in through the curtains.

We shouldn't have had though.

I *should* have been fast asleep, right up until the moment the alarm clock gently woke me with its gradually increasing *'wake up slowly'* light and gentle bird song.

That's if my husband had of spent a bit more on the alarm clock of course.

Instead, it would appear that the cheaper version he chose to buy *isn't* actually 'just the same' as this one wakes you up with an almighty start by flicking its light straight on to a full beam so powerful it penetrates right through your eyelids and with bird song that sounds less like a summer morning and more like the cat's got one of them.

It would have been a more relaxing wake up if the kids had burst in through the bedroom door banging a big bass drum and blowing those screaming party blowers.

You get what you pay for (so my mother keeps reminding me)!

So after months of badgering, my husband, the DIY enthusiast, and I use the word *'enthusiast'* lightly here... he's more the *'I'm not paying THAT for it'* kind of person, eventually got round to buying some cheap black out blinds from Argos and putting them up himself.

Now he does his best.

And I appreciate that.

But his attempt at DIY is... well, let me just say that we're the only household that I know of that has to bluetac its picture frames to the shelves to stop them sliding off.

So instead of paying the street handyman (every street has a 'street handyman') to put them up and who actually charges very reasonable rates -- a few cans of Stella or a half drunk bottle of Bacardi left over from last Christmas -- he decided to do it himself.

I knew it wouldn't go well and sure enough my worst fears were realised when my husband appeared in the kitchen holding a part of the main tubing that even I thought looked a bit too large for him to be holding in his hand.

"Yeah, I cut it a bit too short!"

But apparently it should still be okay as he's managed to bodge it and apparently we couldn't just go and buy another one and then get the street handyman to put it up properly because he's also damaged the window frame trying to screw it in so it's mainly glued.

So in good old, true fashioned, DIY expert style....

He bodged it.

Again!

So I lay there at 6.30am, wide awake with daylight streaming in from around the sides of the blackout blind as it's much too short to cover the whole window.

And not only that but we are only allowed to use it at weekends as it keeps falling down and my husband would rather we use it as little as possible so it might last a bit longer.

Not that that makes any difference at all, as it falls down on weekends too!

But we now have a weekend only blackout blind that is only really ever going to stop any form of daylight from entering the bedroom throughout winter months -- when there's no daylight around anyway.

So I figured if I'm awake again because of this, then it's only fair that he is too.

THUD!

I landed a good one, right between his eyes.

But then made up for it with a snuggle.

Chapter Three

My Daily Life

The husband's entry

"I'm going to write a book!"

My wife looked at me with that... 'Really?!' kind of expression she seems to have perfected over our twenty years of being gently manacled together.

"No, really I am!"

"That was your epiphany?"

The problem I have is that I am actually a very busy man.

It's true, I am!

It's a 100mph whirlwind of stress, activity and shouting just to get the kids (and the wife) up in the morning and out the door for school and work.

Then it's generally a case of avoid all the other 'working from home parents' like me at the school gates and more importantly those 'stay at home parents' that just want to cling on to you and chat forever about nothing at all of any relevance or even importance to me in my daily life and all because they have nothing better to do with themselves when they get back home other than watch Jeremy Kyle so would rather just hang around the school gates waiting for gullible suckers like me to waste their time with because, as my wife puts it, I'm to 'nice' -- hate that word, to tell them I haven't got time to chat so they all cling on to me like viruses desperate for a host.

And so to avoid that daily regime I generally have to drop my kids off at the school gates now in my running gear (with absolutely no intention of actually going for a run) and do that 'bouncing on the spot' thing that jogger's do when they're waiting to cross the road and no one will stop for them while I wave the kids off, and anytime anyone starts approaching from across the other side of the road hoping for a chat mouth the words *'can't stop'* all while tapping the imaginary heart rate monitor on my wrist and simulating that I'm going for a jog by pumping my arms back and forth really fast -- despite still bouncing on the spot.

Or my other ploy is to adopt that Hollywood A-lister approach to not being recognised and wear a baseball cap, shades and a scarf wrapped round my face.

I've even gone as far as a false moustache and sideburns.

But of course it's all a waste of time as they just recognise the kids.

And so as I'm now known around the school as *'that weird dad'* <u>they</u> all avoid <u>me</u>.

So win / win!

Then it's race back home from the school run so I can do my own personal training which normally consists of me going for *'a bit of a bike ride'* (mainly because I can just coast a lot) on my twenty year old mountain bike, which I know is probably not the most practical bike to go riding around the streets on pretending to be some kind of mountain biking Bradley Wiggins equivalent, but as there's nothing wrong with it I really can't justify buying myself a proper *'racing'* bike for the little use it would actually, really get.

Plus it would probably get nicked.

Whereas my old mountain bike is so old if I actually bought a lock for it, it would be worth more than the bike itself.

And so begins the inevitable hunt for my cycling shorts and cycling top in my cupboard draws where they never are.

Then in the airing cupboard.

Then on the radiators.

Before finally finding them still in the dirty wash basket from my last ride and wondering why they haven't washed and ironed themselves before folding themselves up neatly and making their way back into my chest of draws like normal.

And admittedly by the time I'm finished routing through everything, the upstairs looks like we've been burgled as there are clothes strewn everywhere because I start losing patience by the time I get to the airing cupboard and just pull everything out shouting '*I don't have time for this*!' especially as I refuse to ask the wife if she knows where they might be.

And she always does!

And what's all that about anyway?

She'd have known *exactly* where everything was.

I can ask her anything and she'll know where it is?

"Honey, have you seen my spark plug gapping tool?"

"It's in the garage, blue toolbox, left hand cupboard."

It's just incredible.

But it's just the same as never asking for directions.

The shame of it!

The shame of having to admit we don't know where the bloody hell we are.

Or where we're going.

Or running out of toilet paper and being too proud to ask my daughter, who's playing innocently in her bedroom next door, to go and get me one from the downstairs toilet roll storage room (utility room).

So instead I have to sit there, pants round my little ankles, and wait patiently until I can sense there's a clear run from the bathroom to the downstairs toilet roll storage room (utility room) so I can waddle down (relatively) confident of the fact that I won't bump in to the wife, or worse, my son (again -- which was a bit like that scene out of E.T when Gertie sees E.T for the first time and they both freeze, wide eyed and open mouthed and then both run off in the opposite direction screaming), grab a pack of toilet rolls, and then waddle back upstairs again and finish off.

So I end up putting on my swimming shorts which are actually those long Billabong board shorts that my wife thinks are too young for me to still be wearing but that only come out once a year when we go on holiday or maybe the odd occasion when we take the kids swimming when there's NOTHING else to do, and I refuse to pay out on new, more appropriate ones, and a Hong Kong Fuey t-shirt that my kids once bought me as a Christmas present and I have to wear to keep them happy and so that I seem grateful but it's not really the kind of thing that I'd wear out as it makes me look like one of those fully grown men you often see out and about that still thinks it's really cool to wear a superman t-shirt in public aged forty three.

My wife thinks it's really funny to let the kids choose their own Christmas presents for me.

I've unwrapped Power Ranger pants.

A pirate woollen scarf.

Ben 10 mittens.

And of course I have to wear it all.

There's nothing more embarrassing than forgetting you're wearing your Ninja Turtle slippers as you open the front door to sign for a delivery.

And why do they make those things in adult sizes anyway?

So, then I have to hunt around for my cycling shoes which I more than often find outside the back door where my wife has put them as they're usually too wet, too muddy, or both, to come in the house.

Then I have to rub deep heat onto my legs because I read somewhere that that helps the muscles warm up and in my head this saves me from having to do a warm up, which I just don't have the time to do.

Then hunt around for the elasticated support that my wife has now started borrowing to wear on her bad knee when she does her aerobics classes, so that too is never where it should be and is usually in the wash basket but it's so small that I never notice it when I find my shorts.

And if the going's good, and the sun's out, I can (sometimes) hit anything up to ten miles, so on that kind of distance I might have to also consider a bit of Vaseline in the saddle and lower areas that rub together when one cycles.

And of course the nipples!

Well I don't want to get nipple rash from the Hong Kong Fuey t-shirt.

I always smile to myself when I walk in to the bathroom and see my daughter applying the same Vaseline to her lips!

I'll wait till she's in her stroppy teens and then tell her where that's been.

Well she shouldn't have been using my Vaseline should she!

And so by the time this pre-cycling routine is all done, it's normally about two hours later and I've lost all interest in going for a bike ride!

So then I have to sort out any paperwork that might have come through from any late orders the day or night before as that's not going to sort itself out.

Then reply to e-mails.

And I get hundreds of e-mails each day.

Mainly from Nigerian business men that want to offer me several million dollars if I help them to transfer their money out of the corrupt, government controlled bank they currently have it in.

I must admit, if I've not got very much on when one pops up, I do like to have a bit of fun with these.

Filling out all the fields they want you to fill out, but with ludicrously ridiculous details.

Name: Michael Mouse
Address: 1 Disney Land Walk, Florida.

Then offering to fax my house across to them as proof that it does exist when they say they can't find the address.

In the end it gets so ridiculous that *they* just ignore *my* e-mails.

It's a much better way of getting yourself removed from all those SPAM mailing lists.

Or the other regular e-mails I get are from online pharmacies offering me a great deal on penis enlargements.

I even had one offering me a *'two for one'* deal once.

How does that work then?

Or cheap Viagra.

I never really know how to pronounce *'Viagra'* properly.

I mean, is it pronounced v'EE'agra' or is it pronounced v'EYE'agra?

I've also never really understood that southern *'ah'* rule that only those people born down south really seem to understand.

Being northern born and bred I would often make the cardinal sin of daring to ask for a *'glass'* of water without sounding the extra 'A' and silent 'R' -- GLAARSS of water.

I've never been able to find that 'A' and 'R' in any of the southern spellings either.

And, the same (daft) ruling doesn't actually follow suit either.

Glaarss (glass).

Graarss (grass).

Paarss (pass).

PASTA!

There.

No one down south ever says 'PAARSTA' because *'that would just sound weird'*.

GAS!

There's another one southerners!

And don't get me started on 'TOOTH'.

So, then I take care of marketing.

Update the website.

Update the Social Media sites.

Update my *'things to do list'* with things I have to ensure I do because if they're not written down I won't.

Maybe write a blog or two.

You get the picture.

So when my wife questioned how on Earth I was going to fit a *book* in as well....

Well, she probably had a point.

Maybe a *'Time Management Diary'* would be better?

Chapter Four

Those Damn Cats

The husband's entry

"Oh my God, there's a dead slug on the floor!"

A tsunami of noise exploded from the kitchen.

Metal bar stools scraping across tiled flooring.

Falling cutlery bouncing off china plates.

A glass smashing.

The sound of furiously high speed scurrying as the cat's four legs desperately hunted for traction on the laminated flooring from which it sat as it so desperately tried to scamper its way to safety.

Always a funny sight!

I remember once catching the cat sound asleep on the warm bonnet of my car and I thought 'right, time to teach that cat a lesson it won't forget'.

So I crept up to it.

Got really close.

And then….

"WHAT THE HELL DO YOU THINK YOU'RE DOING CAT!"

Well, it jumped a mile, right up in the air, landed back down with all four feet firmly contacting the bonnet of my car and, with claws now out so as to aid traction and a quick getaway and to my absolute horror, proceeded to scratch the living daylights out of my black, swirl free paintwork as its legs moved at over 100mph but its body went nowhere.

33

This in turn made me shout even louder.

"WHAT! OH MY GOD! NOOOOO!"

Which of course just didn't help the situation in any way at all.

"You never thought that one through did you?!"

I span round to see my wife standing in the doorway -- a smug smile on her face as she watched the whole un-thought through proceedings play out.

So at the thought of seeing a dead slug, the kids come skidding into the hallway from the kitchen.

"Whoa, what the...."

"Where, where?"

"What?"

"The slug... where's the slug?"

Now for a brief moment I thought I must have said something like '*Oh kids, I just saw a unicorn trotting across the landing with your mother on its back, her hair flowing radiantly in the wind, surrounded by rainbows*' but oh no, this was a dead... and not just dead, a *crispy* dead slug.

As you've gathered we have a cat.

In fact we have two cats.

Long haired things.

They're a bit of a half breed if I'm being honest.

They should have been the most beautiful Burmese show cats, just like their mother, but apparently her owner left the front door slightly ajar one day as she signed for a delivery and some scraggy old Tom got its paws on her and well... that was that really.

I often get reminded about this story from my father-in-law.

A little *too* often come to think of it.

So, these two half breed cats we have, a black one called Miranda and a ginger Tom called, well, Tom -- along with a few other names I can't print.

He wasn't always called Tom though.

For about seven years of his life he went by another name….

Madison.

I was quite proud of the fact that I had come up with this cool name for the ginger one as my wife and I had agreed that we'd each name our respective cats and naturally these names would stay with them for life, so in my opinion, the more impressive the name the more I could gloat at dinner parties, to be fair.

My wife, *allowed* me to name old ginger Tom, 'Madison' as… well, my previous attempts at naming him weren't quite so exclusive.

"Tom?"

"That's original!"

"Ginge?"

"Right, I'll name them both!"

"NO! No… I'll name him.

So while listening to the Chris Evans Breakfast show on one of my morning drives to work one day I learnt that Chris Evans has a cat called Madison (at least he did have -- not sure if he still has) and I thought, 'that's it – Madison.'

If it's cool enough for Chris Evans's cat then it's cool enough for mine.

Plus, new Madison is also ginger so it had to be fate!

And if my wife doesn't like it, then clearly Chris Evans is at fault and not me.

So with a slight discomforting smirk on her face she agreed that I could call our ginger Tom, 'Madison' and *'yes, your cat's name is so much cooler than mine -- well done!"*

I'd earned myself years of cat name gloating fun!

And the Madison name lasted a while.

A few years in fact.

Up until one day when we were talking to some neighbours outside the house and Madison made his appearance.

"Is this your cat?" the neighbour's wife asked as Madison rubbed around her legs.

"Oh yes, this is Madison." I replied. Smile on my face.

"She's lovely isn't she?!"

The neighbour bent down to stroke him.

"Oh, he's a boy cat." I innocently replied.

She looked up at me….

Turns out Chris Evans cat was female!

And it turns out the name Madison is also female.

Serves it right anyway as we were hosting a dinner party one night, not long after we'd first moved into the neighbourhood.

We wanted to show our immediate neighbours how sophisticated we were.

I had cooked my speciality dishes.

Mushroom soup to start.

All home made.

None of this packet stuff for my guests!

I was supposed to pass the mushrooms through a fine sieve but it was taking too damn long so after about two hours and one dead arm later I just chucked them all in a blender instead.

Same difference if you ask me.

Chicken Fricassee.

This is the only dish I can cook, and is the only dish I ever cook, which is why you never get invited round twice for dinner at our house.

Heart shaped croutons, which had to be gently browned off last minute in the frying pan so they stay crispy but one of the guests decided to pop in and see how I was getting on and then wouldn't stop bloody talking and I couldn't look like I was listening to them at the same time as trying to gently brown off these delicate little things... so they came out black.

And I still served them!

Chocolate mousse.

Which I misread the instructions for and put far too much gelatine in so instead of coming out with peaks resembling the waves of a summers ocean, it set like concrete and the guests had to practically break through their dessert with a hammer and chisel.

And to top it all, while my wife and I were being seen as the perfect hosts, engaging our dinner guests in the most delightful of fruitful conversation, helping to firmly ensure our place on the neighbourhood's score chart of who's hot and who most certainly is NOT hot in the street, the ginger cat scurries past the dining room with something in its mouth.

Now I saw it but pretended not to.

I simply hoped that it would take whatever it had to some remote part of the house, devour it without the guests ever noticing, and that I (or rather my wife) would then deal with the aftermath once everyone had gone.

Of course, life's just not that simple is it?

"Um, I think your cat's just come in with something in its mouth".

"Oh did it? I didn't notice. It's probably just one of its furry play toys. I'll just go and encourage it back outside again."

So I placed my knife and fork down on my plate.

Gracefully set aside my napkin and sashayed off in search of the *bloody cat and its latest mouse*.

From its general directional heading I reckoned it was somewhere upstairs.

Sure enough, the blood trail pointed the way.

Blood trail?

Specks of blood led along the hallway, into our bedroom and under our bed.

I shook my head.

Took a deep breath.

Knelt down.

Slowly lowered my head down to the underside of our bed.

And came face to face with....

A DEAD SQUIRREL!

And it was huge.

Bigger than the cat.

"Are you kidding me cat?! You couldn't just bring in a mouse or even a small bird tonight -- of all nights?"

I could have just flushed that but on no, this had to be disposed of in the outside bin which meant walking it back past the guests.

And, there's no way that this cat, which in all fairness to the cat, is really just one big ginger fluff ball, could have killed this.

The squirrel would have kicked the cat's arse all day long.

I had to give the cat a shower once (long story) and was gobsmacked to discover just how scrawny it actually was without all its bouffant of hair.

No, the squirrel must have died of natural causes and my bloody cat simply scavenged it from the rubbish dump.

And how the hell did it get it through the cat flap?

That must have been a two cat job.

So five minutes later I was walking back past the dining room doorway managing to stop the sophisticated conversation that continues in my absence, dead in its tracks, as I held a dead squirrel by its tail in one hand.

And a ginger cat by its tail in the other.

Which, thinking about it, is probably the real reason that no one ever comes round to one of our dinner parties more than once.

So I'm fairly confident that the slug hitched a lift into our household on the back of old ginge and then somehow managed to drop off.

Which is a God damn miracle as they don't normally and I *normally* have to find myself cutting them free from his long fur while my wife pins him down in some kind of cat half nelson hold while I, donning full protective clothing, goggles and gauntlets, attack him with scissors.

"Where is it Daddy? Where's the slug?"

"In the bin, but leave...."

They tear off towards the office (spare room) and the only decent sized bin in the house.

I follow behind to control the fight that's inevitably about to unfold when my son tries to force my daughter to eat it and my daughter punches him in the face.

"And calm down!"

They stare, cautiously in the top of the bin as if half expecting the slug to jump out at them like those flesh eating slugs in the film Slither.

"Is that it there?"

"No, that's the pencil I broke yesterday. That's it there, look"

My son reaches cautiously in.

Retrieves the dead slug between his thumb and forefinger.

Lifts it slowly up towards the light, turning it round to inspect it carefully.

"This isn't a bush tucker challenge. Put it back and go wash your hands."

"NOW!"

He drops it and they both meander off, back towards the kitchen.

"Cool!"

So the next time they ask me if we can get a dog, a kitten, a hamster, or a lizard, or just something that they promise to look after and spend all their pocket money on until they get bored of it and constantly announce that it's just not fair as they never have time to watch tele or have any money left to spend on comics so I then end up having to feed it, clean it out and spend *my* money on it -- I'll remind them of this and suggest that I get them a dead slug instead, as it'll be a lot easier to look after.

And a lot less expensive.

Chapter 5

Crime Fighting

The wife's entry

So I'm home all alone as the husband has just set off for one of his flying lessons.

He turned forty last year (mid-life) so I guess that says it all really (crisis).

Along with flying he also bought a motorbike.

A 125cc one as he hasn't actually passed his bike test.

He thinks it puts him up there with the cool neighbourhood kids who also all have 125cc motorbikes that the teenage girls all swoon over as they hang around at their gang leader's house that just happens to be across the road from ours, revving their engines all hours of the day and night and all looking like James Dean, but as they're all *actually* seventeen and not a *hundred and seventeen* of course they all just think he just looks like a geriatric old Street Hawk.

Remember Street Hawk, that 1980's series where the cool vigilante motorbike rider would go round dressed all in black solving crimes?

Yeah, well that's as far removed from my husband as you can possibly get.

Yes he's all dressed in black, but the only crime he's solving is '*whose is all this hair in the shower*?' and then determining that as he's the only one in our household whose hair is actually falling out -- it's his.

Or his other common crime solving feat is '*who's hidden my fluffy inner glove warmers*?' and then realising they're warming on the radiator where he left them the night before.

Sooo Hell's Angel!

So while the teenagers in the street are all biking round in shorts, vest tops and looking like a modern day Dennis Hopper in Easy Rider, he wears reflective armbands round his ankles and a fluorescent yellow high visibility vest top over his motorbike jacket so the other car drivers don't miss him.

Not that he needs to worry about any of that as you can always see him coming as there's always a five mile tailback behind him.

He's also started doing all of these extreme adrenaline activities with some of his other 'mid-lifer' friends.

I'm still waiting for the tattoo, earring and boy band haircut to appear.

I often catch him standing in front of the mirror, holding his stomach in, flexing his biceps.

All with a slowly receding, slowly going grey, hair line.

Apparently it's all for me though.

Lucky old me!

So he also started learning to fly helicopters back in January and in his defence he's doing okay.

He's supposed to go solo but our unpredictable British weather keeps putting paid to that.

Last week the cloud base was too low.

The week before it was too windy.

The week before that it was raining -- and it was the 'wrong' type of rain to fly in apparently.

How many different types of rain are there then?

And why don't they just fit windscreen wipers to the helicopter?

His justification for spending (or rather wasting) all of our money on this pointless pastime is that when he passes his flying test we can drive to the airfield, pick up the helicopter and he can fly us both to 'La Manoir' for lunch.

I did also point out that each lesson is the equivalent of one Louis Vuitton handbag by the way, but it fell on selectively deaf ears.

"So if you want to hire one of these helicopters to actually take me to La Manoir, and I'm more than happy to drive there by the way, but the cloud base is too low, or it's raining that 'wet' kind of rain that helicopters apparently can't fly in because they're not waterproof, or it's too windy, or there's a low flying bird at the airfield or whatever reason they can come up with... will they let you actually hire it?"

"No."

"So we can never actually plan anything in advance with it then?"

"Err... No."

Which is just as well as the airfield is actually further away to drive to than La Manoir.

I could never really seem to get my head around the whole solo thing anyway.

Doesn't that just mean he has the laziest instructor?

At no point did my driving instructor say to me *'I'm just going to grab a quick pint in this pub so take it for a spin round the block a few times.'*

The most ironic thing about all of this *'stuck in a metal box at two thousand feet'* business is that he actually has the weakest bladder known to man.

Our days out are pretty much planned around where all the local public conveniences are.

He even has 'Toilet Finder' app on his phone.

In fact they'd made him a coffee during his briefing the other week and he thought it was a bit rude to simply leave it and was so desperate for the toilet half way through a solo flight that he almost brought the Heathrow flight path to a complete standstill trying to land in a field.

So I'm not sure how this whole flying thing is going to go but he seems to be having fun.

Plus, I no longer feel so guilty about buying myself *another* new handbag.

Again!

Chapter Six

Demon Dentist

The husband's entry

I sat, quietly confident, in the dentist's waiting room, my wife next to me.

We were here for our six monthly check-ups.

I hate going to the dentist and he knows it and at the same time I think he gets some kind of sadistic pleasure out of knowing it too.

The last time I sat in his chair he informed me that I needed a filling.

"Here's something to consider, why not let me fill this tooth *without* giving you an injection?"

"What?!"

"No, I'm serious, it's only a small filling and as it's a big tooth it will need a big injection which I think will actually be more painful than the filling."

It's that word isn't it?

PAIN

'More *painful* than the filling'.

Is he serious?

What could be more painful than having your tooth drilled out and then cemented back in again while he's shoving things in your mouth that really have no place being in there and the other one, the dentist's nurse, also getting in on the act and shoving something else in there as well and before you know it you've got more bloody things in your mouth than teeth.

'This isn't a Guinness world record attempt pal. I mean, why don't you go and grab a few patients from the waiting room and see if they can shove a few more things in there as well. In fact, let's just have a party in there.'

I've not had all that many fillings in all fairness.

My mother puts it down to the fact that I was breast fed as a baby and apparently that's supposed to make your teeth and bones stronger.

Really?!

Try telling the hospital where, as a child, I spent most of my time with one thing broken after the other.

In fact I'm surprised I wasn't put into care as I visited the hospital that many times as a kid.

My mother was actually on first name terms with the nurse.

In fact, she came to my wedding.

So I'm sat in the chair and he's just offered me an injection free filling and the only thought that flashes into my mind is that scene from Roadhouse, when Dalton (Patrick Swayze -- one of the coolest damn guys ever to have walked the planet), is sitting on the hospital bed with the incredibly hot blonde nurse (oh, so true to life) and she offers him an injection before she stitches up his knife wound and he refuses it with one of the greatest lines in the whole movie....

'Pain don't hurt!'

So I think... what would Dalton do given this dilemma?

The dentist is there, calling me out.

His sidekick standing next to him with an equally evil looking smile on her face -- goading me.

I'm feeling like a bad guy in a Dirty Harry movie

'*Go on tough guy, make my day!*'

And he actually says -- and I kid you not.

'*What's the worst that could happen?*'

Is he serious?

"Right! Fine. Go on then."

I was half expecting them to clap their hands together with glee and start dancing round the surgery together.

So out comes the drill and it begins.

"If you feel any pain just raise your hand."

Well that hand shot up more times than a Jack in the Box at Christmas time

"I didn't even touch the tooth that time!"

"Well it felt like you did!"

"Well I didn't."

"Is it too late for an injection?"

He backed away.

Stared down at me.

Any thread of respect he once might have had, long gone now.

"Look, I have about three seconds of drilling left to do and then it's done."

And then, and I kid you not, '*She's like the Wind*' by Patrick Swayze plays out of the radio.

I'm not making this up.

Fine --- bring on your last three seconds Mr Dentist.

He did.

And it was bloody painful.

I'd be crap at being tortured.

I'd walk straight in to the torture chamber and tell them everything.

They wouldn't even need to strap me into the chair.

In fact if they made me a nice coffee, one of those white chocolate mocha's you get from Starbucks, and maybe even a skinny muffin on the side, I'd rat out the rest of my troop as well.

In fact my idea of torture, and I mean REAL torture, is turning off the heating because I'm trying to save money and it's about sixteen degrees (yeah, practically tropical) in the house, then forgetting to turn it back on again, and then having to have a luke warm shower.

So, drilling done, and he starts on the other bits while I desperately try to work out what he's doing but have to admit defeat.

Something sucking.

Something blowing.

All the time while the pair of them have this lovely little conversation as they lean across my mouth about her new flat and is she single as he lives with another dentist and he's single and maybe they could all hook up sometime.

Then he asks her how she's finding the surgery and she starts telling him how she had more responsibility at her last practice so he says, 'well here, take over.'

I swear I am NOT making this up.

He passes her that tool, you know the one that gives off that blue light which I haven't got a clue what that actually does and could be his nephew's sonic screwdriver from Doctor Who and he's just having a laugh with her at my expense for all I know, and then he takes the little amber eye shield thing off her and they swap roles.

On me!

'This isn't an apprenticeship scheme pal!'

I thought.

I would have said it but with my mouth resembling the utensils jar in our kitchen I couldn't actually form any words and I feared that any slip of the tongue at this late stage in the game and I'd probably choke.

And I doubt very much if they've have noticed.

So I kept quiet.

I was actually quite proud of myself once it was all over.

I strutted into the waiting room and announced to my wife, in a rather loud voice.

"Yeah, just had a filling and I said, hold the anaesthetic, I'll do it without."

"Really?!"

"Honey -- pain don't hurt!"

I don't know what I was expecting.

A standing ovation from the rest of the waiting patients perhaps?

Anyway I recounted the story of my heroism to anyone that night that would listen, confident that they would all hold me in a much higher esteem now.

"Oh, how funny, I had a filling today as well and also didn't have an injection" piped up the fifteen year old daughter of one of our friends.

"WHAT?!"

"Yeah, they don't really hurt that much do they?"

"What? No....'

Too late.

The damage was done and as the crowd slowly started dispersing , I figured that was the end of my short lived fame.

So, I'm back in the waiting room again for a check up. My wife next to me once more.

I'm confident because I've been flossing *and* I invested in an electric toothbrush with a deep clean setting *and* I've actually been doing the deep clean setting twice in one go.

And I've not been washing the toothpaste out afterwards like I used to do because I read somewhere that leaving the toothpaste in your mouth is better as it helps the fluoride protect against cavities for longer.

Little bit of useful information there for you.

And I bought some of that special toothpaste that costs a hell of a lot more but has something in it that makes it better than all the other toothpastes.

Can't remember what.

"You're a marketers dream, you."

I'll be having the last laugh at our next trip to the dentist I mused.

You see, unlike me, my wife is a bit lapse daisy when it comes to oral hygiene.

She's more interested in getting into bed as quick as she can as the heating goes off thirty minutes before bedtime (I don't see the point of heating the house when you're just going to get into bed), so she sees cleaning her teeth more of a race against the clock.

So we get the call.

She goes first.

Settles herself down in the chair.

The demon dentist leans over with that scratchy, pointy, metal tool thing in hand.

And just to help things along a bit I announce.

"She's not flossing!"

Everyone freezes.

The dentist throws her a look.

"You're not flossing?"

"Oh, thanks a lot!"

"Well she's not -- just thought you should know."

Brownie points for me!

"Well, let's have a look then shall we".

He then proceeds to talk in dentist language and his sidekick starts doodling on a notepad.

I assume she starts doodling because she can't possibly hear what he's saying as he almost seems to mutter it to himself while staring down at my wife's tonsils.

I can't hear what he's saying when I'm actually sat in the chair and he's leaning over me... and she's perched on her stool on the other side of the room.

I actually thought he was calling out bingo numbers at one point and that at any moment she'd shout 'HOUSE!' and wave her note pad in the air.

But I think it's some kind of dentist secret code that allows anyone in the dental profession to talk about their patients while they're in the same room and unless you speak their language you don't actually have a clue what they're talking about.

I went to France once with an old girlfriend.

Other than wearing a striped jumper, beret and a string of garlic around my neck I thought we blended in really well with the foreigners.

Yet we jumped on a busy metro train and found ourselves the butt of the jokes as a train full of teenagers shouted things out in French and the whole train burst out laughing and threw looks our way.

How did they know we were English?

And how did they know we wouldn't have a clue what they were saying?

Guess I just answered my own two questions.

So after about three minutes of calling out bingo numbers my wife was free to go with no follow up action.

I was somewhat disappointed.

"So there's nothing wrong with her? No fillings?"

"Nope, she's good to go."

So I took my place in the electric chair, somewhat let down.

Settled myself in for a quick check and the all clear.

The Bingo numbers started up again... and then they stopped.

His scratchy tool went to work on one of my back teeth.

"Hmmm"

"What?!"

At least that's what I tried to say although it's a bit difficult to be understood with someone's hand in your mouth.

Unless you're a dentist of course, as they seemed to be able to understand the old *'hand in mouth'* language as well.

And why do they always insist on asking you if you're going anywhere nice on holiday this year when you're mouth's being wrenched open so far you'll be lucky if you can ever close it properly again let alone engage him in pointless small talk.

"Yeah, you're going to need a filling."

"WHAT?!"

"This tooth's got a bit of decay in it."

He scratches away some more.

"Well don't make it worse!"

I think.

"But I've been flossing every day. I even bought an electric toothbrush... with a deep clean setting. And I've not been spitting!"

"Well you still need a filling."

I glance across at my wife.

She meets my *'help me out here'* hopeful stare.

Throws back a smirk.

"Poetic justice I think!"

"Oh you're joking!"

And you know what?

I'm sure I *didn't* need a filling.

I'm sure he just couldn't bear to think that he wasn't going to be let loose on my pearly whites for another six months.

Either that or with the amount he charges and the amount of work I have to keep having done, I'm actually the one that's putting his kids through college for him!

Chapter Seven

Best Friends Forever

The husband's entry

I've been invited to watch the World Rally Championships in France this year.

Sounds pretty cool wouldn't you agree?

But here's the thing.

You can throw words at me all day long like….

EXCITING

DANGEROUS

ADRENALINE PUMPING

WHITE KNUCKLE

But really?!

I mean, all those adjectives mean nothing unless you're actually driving the cars.

As a spectator, which is what I'll be, I have some additional words for you to consider….

BORING

COLD

WET

MISERABLE

HANGING AROUND

HUNGRY

TOILET

QUEUE

To be fair, I'm sure if you're into that kind of thing then the first set of words are probably a little more appropriate.

I remember a few years ago attending a business marketing seminar and the guy that ran it actually said to us all….

And I quote….

'You'll never get me playing golf. It has to be the most boring thing in the world and in my opinion ruins a good walk!'

He was of course referring to the fact that everyone's different and what turns one person on may not necessarily float *your* boat but that doesn't matter so you need to make sure you cater for everyone in your marketing.

Which I think is what he meant.

And of course he was totally wrong.

Golf isn't the most boring sport in the world….

Darts is.

And how can that possibly be considered a sport.

I mean, from the little times I watched it (under duress) with my dad when I was a kid, they actually encourage the *'players'* to get pissed.

And don't get me started on snooker!

But at least the three most boring 'sports' in the world have one thing going for them over choosing to drive a full size Scalextric car in circles for the whole of the day….

They have to be a lot less expensive to participate in.

And of course you're less likely to die.

And on that note, if the only reason you're watching motor sport *is* to see an accident -- well, what kind of sick puppy are you?!

Apparently the most viewed time of the Formula One is at the start, when all the crashes happen.

Says it all really.

A bit like the most viewed time of the X-Factor is the audition stage, when all the loons are let out for the day and all seem to turn up, en masse, to sing (massacre) a Katie Perry song.

The general public do love a success story.

But they all love a disaster story much better.

In truth though, I just think that once all the cars have got going, even the hardiest F1 fanatic has to admit that simply watching large go carts do laps of a race track continuously surely must get just a little bit monotonous and so instead switch over to see who's been murdered in Eastender's this week instead.

So, personally I'm not a mad fan of paying to watch someone that I've never met drive a car.

Even if that person does have a really cool name.

In my defence though, I did try the F1 once.

Don't knock it till you've tried it!

I paid the extortionate ticket price.

Took my place alongside all the hardcore race goers wondering with curious interest as to why they were all carrying portable radios with them.

Did they all want to make sure they didn't miss the top 40?

Well, once the cars had all gone out of sight I soon realised why.

So I sat in these very expensive seats (and by expensive I mean they charged way too much for them and not that I treated myself to the posh seats) watching blurred adverts whizz past me at 200mph and not having a bloody clue what was going on.

Occasionally those hardcore regulars would suddenly let out a cheer, or a groan, due to something they'd heard on their radio and I'd have to, once again, call the father-in-law, who was (sensibly) watching it in the luxury and comfort of his own home, to find out what the hell had just happened.

And then, once it was all over, sit in a four hour long traffic jam as a thousand people fought desperately to get out of Silverstone.

And on that same note, once one of the favourites had crashed out, half of the crowd just got up and left.

Even if it was just a few short laps into the race.

Having spent almost £200 to be there, I was planning on staying firmly seated until next year's race.

Biggest waste of time of my life, and trust me, I've had some real serious wastes of times over the years.

So, 'would I like to go to France and watch the World Rally Championships?'

Apparently it's *really* good.

The plan is to head off really early on the Thursday morning.

You know, about three, maybe four AM, to get the first ferry.

Take a steady drive across to wherever in France it's being held.

Watch the qualifying stages, as the build up to the main race is really good fun.

Apparently!

REALLY?!!

Watch the final race.

And then head home Monday morning.

So, five whole days out of my life then eh?!

Not too much to ask I guess.

The problem is I have a real hard time saying '*no*' to people.

Each January I say to myself, '*this is the year I grow a set....*'

And of course I never do.

So as a result, over the years I've done all sorts of things that I really didn't want to do, just because I didn't want to upset anyone.

And also because I'm spineless.

Stag do's where you only really know the stag and he's generally completed pissed at 8am on the first morning anyway and pretty much (thanks to his 'mates') remains that way for the whole time you're there and so you then have to spend a whole weekend in the company of a bunch of alcohol fuelled '*lads*' (idiots) that you don't know, whose sole ambition is to get the stag even more legless, laid or locked up, or all three (the three 'L's), all while they in turn drink themselves into an alcohol induced coma.

Great fun!

And weddings -- in fact this year's New Year resolution is to NOT attend one single bloody wedding.

Not a single one!

Because again, you end up stuck on a table with other people that you don't know because the bride and groom think it might be good to separate you from the only other couple you do know and sit you on a table with a bunch of people you definitely don't know so you can to get to know them so you then have to make small talk about what do they do for a living and where do they live and how funny, I know someone that also comes from there but I won't ask you if you know them as what are the chances of you actually knowing them until it actually kills me to NOT ask them and I drop that line in so many times that eventually I ask and it turns out that, 'no, they don't know Steve Jones from Cirencester'… and why would they?

And then they think you're an idiot for asking as you've just spent the last two hours saying you weren't going to ask.

So I just get drunk and tell everyone I'm a fighter pilot.

Lads nights out, (which is really just a stag do without the stag) with one guy I know and twenty (idiots) that I don't (see Stag do's reference above for more information).

I'm not a big drinker you see and generally custom dictates that on such events you basically have to throw as much beer down your neck as you possibly can as if you're all getting prepared for the world vomiting championships -- which is ultimately what it turns in to for me and the first person to admit defeat (which is usually me) and instead of another vat of Stella, asks for *'just a small glass of orange juice on this round please and maybe some pork scratching as I'm starving… is anyone else hungry or is it just me?'* is considered gay!

Or a wuss.

Or both.

But, on that note, I've discovered a secret weapon.

Becks Blue!

You have to have it in a glass though as the sheer fact that is clearly states 'alcohol free' on the label is a bit of a giveaway and you'd be better off simply drinking coke and telling everyone you're driving as you have to be up early for work the next day (rescuing orphans from burning buildings or something, otherwise you're simply encouraged to 'just call in sick mate!') for the amount of street creed you'll lose if you are caught drinking alcohol free larger.

We hosted a birthday party for my daughter once and one rather colourful mother when offered the obligatory drink asked if we had any lager.

We did.

Becks Blue!

So I poured it in a glass and served it up for her.

She downed it in record time and being the accommodating host that I am, I offered her another.

She downed that.

A third was offered, accepted and downed.

So I offered her a fourth which, surprisingly, she refused on the grounds that she was driving and she was feeling a little bit tipsy.

I know you could be forgiven for thinking that I'm making up a lot of this stuff but seriously, I kid you not, this is the truth.

This fruit loop mom was actually getting pissed on alcohol free larger.

I was really hoping she'd have been stopped by the police and breathalysed.

Could you imagine that conversation?!

So… the World Rally Championships and OH MY GOD -- it's not even one day now!

I could have handled one day (just about).

Many years ago I bought myself an old Lotus Esprit.

Do you remember them?

It was in the days before kids.

Before marriage.

And before anyone could accuse me of going through a mid life crisis.

I had a good job.

Surplus cash

Was still living with the parents.

And I fancied a sports car.

It was also around the same time that Pretty Woman had come out and the lawyer guy lent Richard Gere his, which is how he gets to meet Julia Roberts.

Mine was the same colour as the one in the movie and I felt a million dollars polishing it.

You'll probably note here that I didn't say *driving* it.

It was actually a horrible car to drive.

I bought it second hand -- which in all honesty was about twentieth hand, and I didn't actually get to take it for a test drive before I parted with my hard earned (and just as easily handed over) cash.

I know, I know… but in my defence, the seller wouldn't actually let me test drive it because I wasn't insured.

Turns out he wouldn't let me test drive it because I would have then realised what a bag of nails it was because as soon as owned it, it started constantly breaking down.

Of course it did -- it was a LOTUS

L ots.

O f.

T rouble.

U sually.

S erious.

Plus, I'd get all the boy racers wanting to race me.

I remember finally picking it up.

It was a cold, wet, winter's night.

I pulled up at some traffic lights.

A mate in the passenger seat next to me.

An Escort Cosworth slowly pulled up next to us.

They were quite new at the time and my old knacker really should have been on the scrap heap.

But I didn't care.

It was game on.

Now before I tell you what happened I should perhaps add in that prior to this all my other cars were also old bangers.

Luckily for me I lived on a hill as most of them had to be started not by key....

But by a rolling start.

I had a wheel overtake me once.

I remember thinking 'that looks the same as my wheel' as it flew past, faster than me.

Sure enough it was!

So needless to say that my boy racing experience at this stage was virtually non-existent as not only had I not owned a car fast enough to race anything that didn't need to be pushed, I also never owned anything capable of going fast enough to race anything without my car actually falling apart.

I used to have the local circus owner contact me every six months and ask if he could buy my latest car off me for the clowns to use.

My mate threw a glance across.

"Don't make eye contact," I whispered out of the side of my mouth so the driver in the Cosworth couldn't see.

"Be cool!"

Like I could be cool.

In my head I was Samuel L Jackson in Pulp Fiction.

"Be Cool!"

The reality….

Well… I was just about to find out.

As was my mate.

And everyone else sat patiently at those lights.

'I'll go on amber,' I thought -- get the jump on him.

Plus, this thing's so powerful it'll be like that scene in Back to the Future when all that's left where we once were is a trail of flames.

I dipped the clutch.

Engaged first gear.

Revved the engine.

Stared at the traffic lights.

'Straight ahead. Just look straight ahead. No eye contact,' I thought.

The red lights turned to Amber

I slammed my foot down hard on the accelerator.

The car took off.

Have you ever been on that waltzer ride at the fair ground?

You know that ride that spins round and round incredibly fast and when you try to look up everything simply becomes a blur and you have absolutely no control over anything and all you can do is pray that it will all be over very soon otherwise you'll not only throw up everywhere, but you'll also probably die.

That was us!

"WHAT THE F*~#!!!!!!!!!" screamed my mate at the top of his voice.

All I was waiting for was that dreaded sound of metal hitting metal as I felt for sure that if the Cosworth had done the same as us, we were surely only milliseconds away from a major collision.

But oh no, he was more sensible.

When our ten thousand pound fairground ride had finally come to an end we were facing backwards up a duel carriageway staring face to face with the Cosworth owner.

And his car full of open mouthed mates.

None of the other cars had moved.

And why would they?

The only person that thinks they look cool in a sports car is the numpty driving it.

What a great gift I'd just given them all.

The gift of being able to tell everyone they know that this idiot, poser, in a sports car, almost totalled it and himself... and his mate.

Thank God 'You Tube' was still another fifteen years away!

But it didn't end there.

Oh, no!

I then had to try and make a three point turn in a Lotus Esprit that despite being British, is really too low and too wide for British roads, and... you can't actually see out of any of the windows, particularly the one at the back as someone, the designer I guess, who has clearly never, ever, sat in a lotus, thought it would be a good idea to build a letterbox into the rear of it, fill it with glass and call it a rear window.

Plus, they then add a spoiler which completely obscures any possible view you might have had out of it anyway.

Crunch! -- I backed into the curb.

"Oh you're KIDDING ME!"

"Mate, can we just get out of here?!"

"Are you serious? Can you not see I'm BLOODY TRYING!"

So at some point I must have mentioned to my 'inviter' who, I can't actually call a friend because to be honest he's not.

He's simply the *'stay at home'* dad of a kid that's in the same class as one of my kids.

We've NEVER spent any time together.

EVER!

And suddenly, here I am getting invited to spend the whole weekend with him.

People are really strange sometimes.

Or perhaps it's just me.

I got invited round to some bloke's house once, again, didn't really know him, to join him for a few beers in his new hot tub.

Really?!

Are you really asking me to come round to your house, strip off to my pants and then lounge around in your hot tub together drinking beer and accidentally touching flesh every now and again?!

And the only real reason to do so is because *'it's new'*?

I wouldn't dream of saying to him *'just had a new bathroom fitted, fancy coming round and taking a bath with me?'*

Or trying out the new toilet together?

And why can't we just drink them in your lounge instead?

Or better still... just go to the pub?

With other people!

So my wife and I have a rule now.

If I ever get asked on a play date I immediately turn to her and say *'hey honey, this guy that I don't know all that well wants to spend some time with just me and him and no one else… are we doing anything on said date?'*

And she….

If she's not in one of her funny 'ha ha' kind of moods, generally replies with '*Oh, what a shame, we're off to Centreparcs that weekend.*'

And we're generally at a wedding the following weekend.

Then there's my operation.

Then my grandad's funeral.

Again.

And then they finally give up.

Or just get the hint.

And all without me ever having to upset or offend anyone.

So at some point I must have said something like… '*Oh you have a Porsche? I used to have a Lotus'.*

And so that was that.

We're now best mates.

And I find myself desperately thinking of another reason why I can't make the bloody World Rally Championships *again* this year.

The cruncher though is that we'll be taking his Porsche and if I pay for the extra on the insurance he'll add me on as a temporary, additional driver.

Now were it a 918 I'd have said '*sod it*' and gone in a heartbeat.

I'd have almost considered it if it was a 911.

But it's not.

In fact it's far from it.

It's a 924.

I'm really sorry if you've ever owned one but let's face facts, the 924 was NEVER cool.

Back in the day it was the car for people that couldn't afford a proper Porsche.

And whether his was ever a new one I don't know but he's got one now.

All one thousand pounds worth of it.

We'll never get there!

So me being me, I feign my usual pretend interest and say *'yeah that sounds great, tell me some more about it'*.

"You're doing what?!"

My wife kills herself laughing.

 "Camping! We're camping together! In a two man tent!"

"You know what that means don't you? That means you'll be sleeping in the same bit. Next to each other."

"Centreparcs! I'll just tell him we're at centreparcs!"

"You can't use that one again!"

"I bloody can. Either that or I've got a brain tumor!"

So my wife thinks I'll have a great time.

Me, I just think clearly this dad hasn't got any other mates he can invite.

Surely he doesn't think that because I too once owned a knackered old banger of a sports car we have something in common.

Perhaps that's what it is.

Perhaps the fact that he drives around in a two-seater, Porsche 924 while his family follow behind in the family car is the real reason he has no one else to ask.

Or perhaps it's because he wears a knitted jumper with a picture of his 924 sewn on the front to the school pick up.

I don't know.

All I do know is that because my wife doesn't think I should tell him I have a highly infectious and incurable disease....

And because I've exhausted all other possible and more importantly... believable excuses....

Come next October I'll be snuggling up in a two man tent next to a guy that I really know nothing about while rally cars scream round a track to the shouts of spectators baying for an accident, all while trying desperately to drift off to sleep having just spent the whole day drinking nothing but Becks Blue, desperately needing the toilet but too scared to move in case I disturb him and he decides to spoon with me and all while as he poses around in his 924 and knitted jumper looking really cool in the daytime.

And everyone thinks I'm his mate.

Let's just hope he never buys a hot tub!

Chapter Eight

Our Little Flower

The wife's entry

"Ask your daughter what lunchtime school club she's signed herself up for."

My husband kicks back in his office chair as I dump the school bags, coats, shopping (bought on the way to pick up our daughter) handbag all onto the hall floor, shoo the cat back outside and close the front door.

Now you have to picture our daughter.

She's eight years old.

With golden brown hair that flows delicately down her back.

Green eyes that shimmer mesmerizingly in the summer sun.

She's tiny.

Petite in fact.

She's caring.

She loves animals.

She loves people.

Her hobbies include making things out of empty cereal boxes (and using up all the sellotape in the house).

Drawing.

She draws hundreds of pictures of the family with little notes attached telling us how much she loves us.

We'll often wake in the morning to find yet another of these stuck to our bedroom door.

We don't need to decorate anymore.

Anytime we want to change the look of a room we just need to buy her a present.

My husband likes to save all the pictures -- what for I don't know.

If he keeps saving them at the rate he currently does we'll have to move to a bigger house, just to have somewhere to keep them all.

She loves dancing.

She loves singing.

When she's not writing notes she's dancing and singing her way around the house.

She's definitely going to be an entertainer one day.

And she loves being nice!

Apparently that is a hobby.

A *nice* one.

So as I hang up the coats my husband feigns interest as he tends to do when he's in the middle of doing another important thing on the computer which looks to me like he's really just prioritising his rental list on LoveFilm.com.

He loves watching movies.

He'll watch anything no matter how bad it is.

We watched a film called 'Buried' once because one of his mid-lifers told him it had a great twist at the end.

The twist being, of course, that someone actually sat through the whole of it.

So we sat down to watch it and within three minutes I knew it was time for a trip to the late night petrol station to pick up some newspapers, but he of course stuck with it.

An hour into it and I had to ask, "Is it just him in a box for the whole film?"

"No, this is just the set up stage. It'll get going in a minute."

"Well it needs to get going as that's what I'll be doing as so far it's just him in a box with a lighter and, conveniently, a mobile phone".

Who buries someone in a box in order to kill them, and then leaves them a lighter to help them see and a mobile phone that they can call people on?

It's like those James Bond films when the villains straps 007 on to a metal table and a laser beam slowly cuts through the metal as it makes its way (very slowly) towards his nether region.

Now I'll be the first to admit that I'm no criminal master mind but I do know enough to know that if I was a super villain and wanted someone dead I'd probably consider something a little quicker and possibly even a little more certain.

Like shooting him for example!

All taken care of in an instant.

No worry of him escaping, hunting me down and then exacting his revenge!

Which *ALWAYS* happens.

And forgive me for sounding a bit stupid, as I don't know much about shooting someone, but I assume it's more effective than all of the other *'ways to Kill James Bond in order to drag the movie out, give us all some suspense, and of course allow him enough time to either get rescued or work out a way to escape which we know he's going to do anyway (otherwise they would have just shot him) so any attempt at the director putting us in a state of heightened suspense is completely negated by this small fact'.*

Plus, the super villain is so intelligent he can create a super hideout buried deep within a mountain but can't work out that it would be better to just drop Bondy in the vat of acid and be done with it as opposed to rig up a very cleverly designed (and no doubt quite expensive) contraption that lowers him into it very slowly.

And how has he got any mobile phone coverage in that box anyhow?

We live on a normal residential housing estate in a respectable part of the country and my bloody phone doesn't get service unless you sit on the roof of the house holding an unravelled metal coat hanger high into the air all whilst dressed in a silver foil suit.

So an hour and a half into it and we've still not met anyone else and guess what... he's still in the box.

But to add the much needed drama and suspense, his lighter's running out and his battery is getting low.

Who cares!

"Yeah, I'm beginning to think that perhaps it's just him in a box."

I say nothing more until the very end of the film when... and here comes the spoiler alert -- he dies.

"Well what a pile of shite that was!"

"What? No, it was very cleverly done actually."

Which I interpret to really mean *'yeah you're right but I can't admit to you dear wife that we've just wasted an hour and forty five minutes of our lives as your look of 'I told you so' would just be far too much for me to have to deal with, as well as coming to terms with the fact that this film was actually crap'.*

"Anyway, this *'Open Water'* movie looks quite good so I'll order that for next weekend to make up for it.

Open Water was just as bad as that other film he made us sit through about Robert Redford being shipwrecked at sea and just as he's about to drown himself, just as you finally think 'THANK GOD' because I'm all set to bloody drown him for agreeing to do such a crap film...he gets rescued.

Who lights a fire on an inflatable life raft anyway?!

I mean what was he thinking?

There was only one word spoken throughout the whole of that film...
the 'F' word, which sums up how I pretty much felt when it had ended.

So now we have a deal.

He doesn't moan about the fact that we're not sharing the experience together when I take a little cat nap next to him....

And he can watch all the zombie films he wants.

He watches most of these films through an app on our smart TV.

I have to say, I struggle to keep up with the apps on my mobile phone let alone the TV thinking it can get in on a piece of the action as well.

And when did TV's become *smart* anyway?

And why do they need to be?

We didn't actually need a smart TV but another of his mid-lifers works in the trade and got him a good deal on it so we actually had to sell the other perfectly good one and for half the price we paid for it just eight months earlier at that, just to have somewhere to put this new one.

You can wave your arms about in front of it and it will do things.

Change channel.

Lower the volume.

That kind of thing.

It never works of course.

And you can talk to it.

Although that works about as well as the talking sat nav system we paid extra to have fitted into our car.

"Navigation, Go Home."

"Navigation, Japanese Restaurant, please say 'enter destination or start route guidance."

"What? No! Cancel! CANCEL!"

"Starting route guidance now."

You can tell the TV to turn on just by saying '*TV, turn on*'.

And he tries.

He tries and he tries and he tries.

I have to hand it to him -- he's not a quitter my husband.

"TV, turn on."

"TV switch on."

"Hi TV, switch on."

"Hi TV, please turn on."

So while by husband tries in vain to chat up the TV and the kids sit silently staring at the still black screen, I simply walk into the lounge, pick up the remote that lays right NEXT to him and turn the bloody thing on myself before heading back into the kitchen to continue chopping up the carrots.

In fact it actually comes with two remote controls.

One normal looking remote and one fancy remote with a swipe pad that does 'extra stuff' that I apparently 'don't need to worry about as it would be far too complicated for me to understand', which simply means -- he doesn't have a clue.

Now why you need two remote controls for one TV I don't know but he never uses the second one with the swipe pad because 'it doesn't actually work very well' which I think is just actually in keeping with this overly expensive and totally unnecessary TV we (he) bought.

So just recently I've started waiting for them to all settle in the lounge, popcorn in hand, and then I sneak up to the lounge door, wait for him to utter those inevitable words and then like Ali Baba and 'open sesame' I hit the 'ON' button and like magic the TV fires into life and my husband receives a round of applause from our very easily impressed kids.

It doesn't end there though.

We used to have Sky TV but they increased the fees by something like one whole pound a month and in true 'tight arsed' form he got rid of it because he wasn't paying THAT each month for it 'and we never watch the TV anyway'.

The truth is that he spent so much time flicking through the thousand channels we all now have that by the time he actually found something he wanted to watch I was fast asleep and it was time for bed.

So as I make my way back from the shoe cupboard towards the office my husband's still holding his arms out waiting for his delicate little flower to run into them, once she can get her buckles undone.

I give her a little helping hand and she darts off, throwing herself at him and kissing him all over his face.

He laughs and tickles her and she goes all giddy which makes him do it even more.

"Daddy stop it! Stop it daddy!"

"Only if you tell me what school club you've sign up for."

"Okay, okay I will!"

He stops tickling her.

Sits her on his knees.

Looks lovingly into her dazzling green eyes.

"So what have you signed up for princess? Flower arranging? Sewing club? Swimming perhaps?"

"No daddy -- TAG RUGBY!"

Chapter Nine

KIDS!

The husband's entry

KIDS!

Kids, kids, kids!

As you've probably gathered I have two.

Little cherubs.

I do my best to avoid them.

Stay out of their way.

But for some reason they just keep hanging around.

Funnily enough my wife thought it would actually be a good idea for me to write this book as she thought it might help me with some of my... 'challenges'.

Therapy if you like.

Not sure what she means.

In my head, I *am* the 21st century dad.

Although she doesn't seem to think I'm going to win any father of the year awards.

And neither do they.

And I have to say... they probably have a point.

You see I'm the kind of father that could probably be called, by some, *'a bit immature'*.

Whereas I would call myself… *'fun!'*

I don't see what's wrong with encouraging your two your old to go snuggle up on his sleeping rug and have a nap -- and then when he does, seeing how many things I could balance on him before they fell off.

Or he woke up.

As if that wasn't bad enough, my wife thought that the fact I then photographed my triumph (almost to the ceiling -- quite an achievement) and posted it on Facebook was going a bit too far.

I thought I'd make *'Baby Jenga'* the new *'Breaded Cats'* (Google it).

In all fairness to me though, I do my best.

And on a serious note, I actually think my kids are pretty cool.

I mean, what father doesn't?

And we do have a load of fun together.

In fact, it's actually a laugh a minute if I'm being honest.

Well it is when we look back at least.

Falling off the footstool that he shouldn't have been climbing on in the first place and flinging the toy car he was clutching through the lounge window on his way down in a last bid attempt to save himself, wasn't that funny at the time.

It is now though.

And stuffing all his pants down the toilet then flushing it causing it to all overflow and leak through the bathroom floor and consequently the kitchen ceiling wasn't that funny at the time either.

Neither was the plumber's bill.

Or the decorator's.

In fact, come to think of it, it still isn't that funny.

My son's ten now and a tad more... under control, shall we say.

And I feel that I've had a big part to play in that education.

Whereas my daughter is eight and God knows how she's made it to that milestone without killing herself.

We're on first name terms with the nurses in the A&E department.

A little bit like I was when I was her age funnily enough.

We've actually sponsored a bed for her.

It's not that she's clumsy.

She's just very... *daring*.

And probably clumsy.

The best way to describe her is that she doesn't so much *slide* down a slide.

No.

She *launches* herself down it.

Flings herself down things.

Stairs.

Paths.

Driveways.

Holes.

If you looked up the word *liability* in the dictionary there'd be a picture of her.

Now you'll probably be saying *'hang on, earlier you said that she was the cutest thing'.*

And it's true, she is.

But then so was Chucky when he wasn't possessed.

Only joking.

And she's a tad forgetful.

And I say 'tad'….

We had to pull her out of school at lunchtime once for a dentist appointment.

My wife wrote a letter to her class teacher informing her that she would pick up our daughter at lunchtime.

My daughter had been briefed to meet us at the school gates where she could simply jump in the car and we could then shoot straight off to save us having to drive into the school grounds and run the risk of killing a child as they no doubt throw themselves in front of the car.

And it all went like clockwork.

Until we arrived at the dentist that is and my wife casually roots through my darling daughters school bag looking for the usual school letters or homework assignments while we wait in the reception area.

And pulls out the letter.

So as far as everyone's concerned we've not only illegally nabbed our daughter from school but more importantly we've also failed to gain anyone's consent either.

And, as my wife carefully points out, failed to inform anyone that she would be missing for the rest of the day as well.

I go outside to make a quick phone call as my wife smiles awkwardly at all the eyes now firmly fixed on us.

So as you can imagine we're forever getting called from her school telling us things like, 'she's forgotten her P.E Kit', 'where's her homework?' and 'her dinner money hasn't been paid for the past three days' -- again.

It's in her school bag for God Sake!

All you have to do is ask her for it.

But guess what... they're not allowed.

That's right....

They're not allowed to ask her for it -- apparently.

I think it has something to do with the latest policy thing the schools have.

One more reason the country is in the 'unfortunate' state it's in.

Don't get me started!

So instead, they waste even more time phoning me up.

Luckily they still feed her though.

But at least it's a modern day school they both go to.

For example, one of the most important things they do is teach children their rights.

From aged four.

I found this out when my son came home one day and informed us that it was his right not to eat his cabbage.

He soon came around to the idea when I informed him that it was my right to give it him for breakfast.

My daughter does a little modelling work -- see, told you she was quite cute (plus that new motorbike fund isn't going to fill its self up now is it?!)

And so for this you have to get a licence -- something to do with kids working.

I don't really know as the wife tends to deal with all that *'kids stuff'*.

Now she had a job recently and it was a last minute thing so as it takes around five days, a solicitors letter, the deeds to your house, your last will and testament and a sample of your DNA just to get a licence, and if you know anything about the world of modelling, which we didn't, but are now experts in, you'll know that most jobs come up last minute.

Meaning there's never enough time.

A client calls up a modelling agency, asks them if they have someone available for a shoot and normally those shoots are in a few days time and so there the problem starts.

So we started the ball rolling with the licence but on this one off occasion it was too short notice and because it was for a good job and blah, blah, blah we said she could do it.

So she did.

Yes, a little naughty of us but what's the worst that's going to happen?

I mean, it's not like she's missing trigonometry or anything -- she's eight, remember.

And then we got the phone call from the school telling us they wanted to see one of us.

'I told you this would happen,' I said, in my best *'I told you this would happen'* voice. *'You made the decision. It's in your hands now. Nothing to do with me!'*

I've become quite the expert when it comes to squirming out of my responsibilities.

But in my defence, over the next few hours we both worked together to come up with all the varying and justifiable reasons for our crime.

We even role played the meeting.

Me, playing the female, whisky drinking (I just assume this of course as she's always a little too jolly for first thing in the morning and also has a constantly bright red nose which, to the best of my knowledge isn't because she likes to take part in Christmas related, reindeer type re-enactments at weekends), head teacher as she throws those curveball questions out and then going over the best possible and least incriminating (prison sentencing) answers.

Took us all morning to get our story right.

And in our defence, my daughter is quite the athlete and is *always* being pulled out of lessons to represent the school for cross country races or swimming events and even as I write this she's in that school tag rugby team tournament my wife mentioned earlier.

I mean seriously....

She hasn't even had a lesson yet and they've got her in the team.

She's one of only two girls in a boy's team.

I don't think it's because she's that good.

No, I think it's more to do with the fact that there was no one else that wanted to do it.

In fact, I've literally just got off the phone to my wife who is at the match (freezing cold) and her school is through to the semi finals.

I'm especially proud of her as she apparently did a great tackle on a boy twice her size.

She launched herself at him so hard that she ripped his top, dragged him to the floor and sat on him.

His father went mad apparently, dragged him off the pitch, and took him home.

It's true -- I'm NOT making this up!

"Daddy, the man said lots of rude words at me."

"Good for you then!" I said, until my wife informed me that she was only actually supposed to steal the tag from his belt and not half kill him.

She does get a little carried away sometimes!

Plus, her school does do very well at these kind of sporting events, often coming in the top three.

And this is all okay.

She's allowed to miss lessons for this.

And generally on the last few days of term they're allowed to take games in to play so again, there's no lessons taking place.

But you try to take your kid out of school to start their holiday a day early and my God is there an uproar.

Which is why most kids that are off sick at her school normally return a week later with a tan.

Anyway, don't get me started on this either.

So my wife sloped off to the meeting with the headmistress and I hid anxiously at home, waiting for SO19 to scream up outside, boot the door down and hurl me into the back of a riot van.

Half an hour later she was back.

I nervously greeted her at the front door, bracing myself for the heavy fine we were surely to receive or even worse, the news that our crime was so heinous we'd have to look for another school for her.

"Well?!"

With baited breath I awaited the response.

My wife threw me a glance.

Then announced the news that, knowing my daughter as I do now, even I was not quite expecting.

"She pulled down a girls skirt in the lunch queue!"

And the worst thing... the school weren't calling us about that.

Or even to tell *us* off as the bad parents we must be for raising a daughter that could do something like that.

Oh no.

They were calling us in to *ask our permission* to *speak* to her about it.

Ask our permission!

What has this world come to?

I remember getting the slipper at school for just walking across the climbing frame area.

Not even climbing on the climbing frame.

Just crossing some of the tiles that the climbing frame was built on.

And why?

Because you weren't allowed in the climbing frame area if it wasn't your class's turn.

That was it.

Real Victorian standards in my day!

And it turns out it wasn't just her either.

Apparently there was a craze, which by all accounts only lasted a day, where it was considered funny to pull down someone's skirt.

It's just the girl whose skirt my daughter pulled down didn't actually find it all that funny and instead stood her place in the lunch queue, tray in outstretched hands, screaming hysterically, skirt round her little ankles and bloomers on full show while my daughter squatted down, still clasping the downed skirt, red faced, and desperately trying to act like she didn't do it.

Guilty as charged!

And so that was that.

The head teacher called my daughter, along with pretty much all the kids in the school, into her office and told them *'not to do it again'*.

But you have to love the schools really.

They do try to get it right.

We had to attend the *'your kids starting school so in you come for a nice friendly meeting with people that smile a bit too much for my liking'*... kind of meeting.

We were briefly informed as to what to expect from the school in the way of signposting this and signposting that and then we were introduced to the school counsellor.

Not the school counsellor like they had in my day, that gave you (rubbish) careers advice.

Apparently I was destined to drive an ice cream van which ruined my plans to be an astronaut.

No, the person that would offer your four year old psychiatric counselling if they needed it.

A shrink for kids basically.

Now I get that in this day and age we've managed to put labels on kids for the way they behave which in the olden days (how old do I sound?) that child would have simply been branded as *naughty*.

And not wanting to be politically incorrect here but I can, kind of see, how some kids might *not* just be *'misunderstood'*.

I mean there are kids in some of the after school clubs that my kids go to with conditions that I can't even pronounce, let alone have even heard of.

And some of those conditions have also been self-diagnosed by their parents.

Parental diagnosis.

"Yeah, he has ADHD, that's why he's tearing up your sports hall."

"Oh, that's what's he's been officially diagnosed with then is it, by a specialist?"

"No, that's just what I think."

As he downs his second can of Red Bull.

Forget spending years training up to be considered expert enough to actually recognise these conditions... and then of course credible enough to be able to diagnose them.

It's a bit like those self serve tills in the local supermarkets.

Or the self service petrol pumps.

Self-diagnosis -- it's the latest thing.

Or self-labelling.

I did one of those stupid mud run style assault courses once.

Don't ask me why, it just seemed like a good idea at the time, which of course it would have done six months before I actually had to do it -- which, incidentally, is way long enough to realise those crucial thoughts that were clearly missing at the time of clicking submit -- 'what the hell am I thinking?!'

If it wasn't for the fact that it had cost me almost a hundred pounds I wouldn't have turned up, but me being me, I couldn't let that one go either.

So I did it.

And even just before the start of the race, the MC informed us that 'we're going to be swimming through loads of dirty, muddy, rat urine infested water and we'll most likely swallow a load of it and if any of us feels a bit ill after, head down to your local quacks, tell them you've been swallowing rats piss and they'll sort you out'.

Lock you up more like!

And sure enough, that very night I find myself on my knees, head over the toilet, throwing up with such violence it was unlike any hangover I had ever had.

All night.

Vomit everywhere!

What the hell do those rats drink?!

That bloody river water by the way I was feeling.

So the next day I head off down to the local doctors surgery, give her my symptoms and get this... she punches it all into Google.

I even watch her doing it.

"So what are your symptoms?"

"Well, I did this mud run (typing) and swam through a river (typing) and think I swallowed some of the water (typing) and I've spent the whole night throwing up."

"Yeah, it says here you have Weils Disease."

Well thank you Doctor Kildare! You've certainly earned your £100K a year haven't you?

I could have done that... at home!

"Oh and it also says to next time drink a can of full fat, flat coke after and that should stop it happening again."

REALLY?!

Does it?!

Not wanting to be outdone, my son's school introduced a 'Buddy Bench' system where any child that doesn't have a friend to play with during any break time could simply head over to the buddy bench, sit down and a group of other kids would instantly come skipping over and invite them to play.

You know, not a bad idea really.

It beats family psychology time.

And my son was / is quite popular with all the other kids at school so never really had many real problems playing with other children -- except on this one, rare occasion.

"So who did you play with at school today son?" I innocently enquired.

"No one."

"No one? Why, what happened?"

"Everyone was already playing."

"So, did you go and sit on the buddy bench then?"

"I would have done except for one thing."

"And what was that?"

"It was full."

They even had TWO buddy benches, which at the time I thought was a tad unnecessary.

Turns out it wasn't enough for those dopey kids.

My daughter come out of school once and informed us that the ambulance came into school today with its lights flashing and siren going and whipped three kids off to hospital pretty damn quick.

Quite a drama for all the kids and certainly a major talking point.

Turns out that some kid threw up which the teacher then cleaned up, naturally… but unlike in my day when they just threw some sawdust over it and left if for the poor old cleaner to deal with later that night, nowadays they use some special chemical to clean it off the carpet with so that the smell doesn't make all the other kids in the classroom throw up as well and this chemical apparently froths up and looks a bit like snow and three of those kids decided to get down on their hands and knees when the teacher wasn't looking and lick it.

Not, *touch it,* which you could, perhaps, for a brief moment, *almost* understand, especially if they thought it *was* snow.

No….

Lick it!

And before you ask '*why the hell didn't the teacher barricade the area off?*'

She did, but those daft kids were so desperate to suck up chemicals, they just clambered over it!

Guess that's their future all sorted then.

And no wonder they offer the kids shrinks at her school.

But the schools simply make it worse for themselves as they try desperately to be, oh so *politically correct* and *health & safety* conscious while at the same time allowing the kids to exercise their human rights.

And in its defence, my kid's school does try its best.

The have a fantastic disciplinary system.

Basically if a child is naughty, they move their name from a smiley face section of the black board to a sad face section of the black board.

BRILLIANT!

This is obviously going to stop any naughty behaviour dead in its tracks.

After all, the thought of having their name taken from the smiley face bit and stuck under the sad face bit is enough to stop any would be future serial killer.

It's a bit like those police reality shows I occasionally watch where the repeat offender car thief that has just nicked some poor bugger's pride and joy and smashed up half the town in it almost killing a load of innocent members of the public in the process is finally caught by the police and as we wait with baited breath for the judge to place the black hankie on his bonce and bring back capital punishment, all he actually gets as just and fair punishment for his unspeakable crime is an *additional* two years on top of his current two year driving ban.

Well brilliant!

Well done Your Honour, that's really going to stop him as it clearly made all the difference last time you banned him.

And of course, naturally all the kid's slates are then wiped clean each night so they all start again the next day with a smiley face.

Like a kind of naughty Etch-A-Sketch.

A friend of ours was moving her child into the upper school and being the concerned parent she was enquired as to the processes in place for dealing with disruptive children.

She learned that they actually have a great working policy in place.

They simply let the kids carry on until they've finished as they're not actually allowed to restrain them unless they've done the course -- which most haven't.

I'd love to sign up for that course.

What do you suppose it's called *'Six week course on how to restrain kids -- sign up now!'*?

And this *'no hands on'* approach works brilliantly apparently as one proud teacher informed her that one particularly disruptive child has only smashed the classroom up twice this term.

Needless to say she took her kid elsewhere.

But I do get all this *'political correctness'*.

All this *'child protection'* stuff.

But, and I'm not being funny here, I don't always think it's actually the children that need protecting from their parents.

No!

It's the parents that need protecting from their children!

Chapter Ten

Boris Johnson

The husband's entry

I do love motivational quotes.

We used to have those cool, framed, Athena posters in the office where I used to work (back in my youth) that used to preach motivational quotes at you all the time.

'NEVER GIVE UP -- go over, go under, go around or go through... but NEVER give up' and the poster would be some guy at the top of a mountain.

Brilliant!

Anytime you were feeling a little de-motivated in that *high pressure, commission only, everyone hates you, how did you get this number, don't you ever call me again, I'm going to kill you and your family,* telesales job, you need only glance up briefly and you would be instantly re-charged and ready to pick up the phone once more and listen to some out of work, lazy arse tell you what he was going to do to your mother if you ever phoned him again.

Thank God video calling never took off!

And really... what was the company actually thinking anyway?

'Here's a list of people's home phone numbers for you to call today and when they answer, sell them a two hundred pound mobile phone, plus a thirty pound connection charge, plus a tariff that they'll spend more on to run in one month than they would on their home phone throughout the whole year and you have to sell at least twenty of them -- TODAY!'

Well I've got news for you Big Business... back then, before all this *'yeah, I'm working from home today, let's do a conference call'* nonsense, there was only one type of person that was at home in the daytime and consequently able to answer their home phone….

THE UNEMPLOYED!

And the only reason I took the job in the first place was because I was conned into it.

"Yeah, you'll be an account manager and manage your own accounts and everything."

"Great, and will I get a company car as well?"

"Errr… yeah!"

I didn't!

In fact I turned up on the first day having just gone through the biggest shock to the system ever -- a train journey into London on a Monday morning.

I remember, bouncing in to the old derelict warehouse they called an office with a big smile on my face ready to be handed all these accounts to manage and the only thing I was handed was a bloody great Yellow Pages.

Do they still actually print those by the way?

At least they gave me some on the job training though.

"Turn to 'A' and start dialling!"

I lasted two weeks.

And even now I can't fathom how the hell that guy in all his climbing gear at the top of that mountain actually had anything to do with selling mobile phones.

I would have found all those poster far more motivational if there had been a photo of some homeless guy, laying in his own urine, drunk off his face on tenants extra at eight in the morning and the slogan read *'If you don't pick up the phone and sell something, this will be you next Monday!'*

Do you remember Athena?

That cool, poster shop that, as a teenager in the eighties we all used to love going in and browsing through all the hundreds of posters they'd have on display in those metal frames that resembled a huge metal book.

There were hundreds of them, remember?

If you flicked through enough of the crap ones you might eventually get lucky and come across some hot looking model in a swim suit.

It was kind of like a poor man's internet.

Anyway, as no one really wanted pictures of dogs dressed as people or cute looking babies in a flower pot it didn't last all that long as I seem to remember.

Or was it simply because the internet actually got invented which consequently eradicated the need to make that long journey to the shop when you could simply just lock yourself away in the bedroom with your laptop.

Far simpler!

I often wish I could come up with some of my own, unique, awe inspiring, motivational quotes that haven't already been said.

Or maybe even just something philosophical.

I'd make a fortune!

I keep practicing all my quotes on the kids.

"Remember kids, if you reach for the moon and fail, you'll still land in the stars!"

Two blank faces stare back at me

"Do you know what that means?"

I meet their gaze -- hopeful.

"Either of you?"

My wife shakes her head and goes back to her newspaper.

"Well?"

"What was the question again?"

And so that's about as philosophical as I get.

So I can only assume that something, a gene perhaps, has kind of rubbed off on my son.

Either that or he's been browsing through Athena online (yes, there is one -- I double checked!).

"Dad can I have a horse?"

"No!"

"Can I have a dog then?"

"No!"

"What about a cat?"

"We've got two already -- have one of them."

"How about a rabbit?"

"No."

"A chinchilla?"

"A Chinchilla? What are you gay?"

"How about a lizard?"

I went through a bit of a rebellious stage as a teenager.

Well for me it was rebellious.

You see I was never one of those eighties kids that got their ear pierced.

I never had a Keegan perm.

I never had a tattoo.

Still don't, although back then tattoos were never really as popular as they seem to be now.

The only people with tattoos when I was a teenager were really hard men, and then they'd all just have the stereotypical anchor or 'MUM' tattooed on their forearm.

Tattoos today have become an art form.

Fashion even.

I have a friend, a female friend, that just loves tattoos.

Apparently it's addictive?!

She's so far had most of her body tattooed and is currently in the process of having one done that covers the whole of her back.

She showed me the work in progress recently.

Apparently you can have them done in stages which is very helpful for her as she doesn't have that much money and so has to keep saving up to have the next bit done.

She's spent a few hundred pounds on it already and when it's completely finished it will have cost her over a thousand pounds and to be honest, to me, it just looks like she's fallen asleep and her three year old has got hold of a permanent marker.

And it's going to look great on the beach!

Now I know I'm considered *'old fashioned'* at this middle aged stage of my life but I just keep thinking, that could have been a nice weekend away for her and her family!

And if I didn't have much money, I'd certainly consider spending what little I had on something a little more... beneficial.

But that's just me.

We have some more friends that constantly plead poverty and yet have a cleaner and an ironing lady.

And to pay for those extravagancies, when the husband isn't at his main job, he has to work part time as a cleaner for someone he knows with a big house.

A CLEANER!

So he can pay for the cleaner that cleans his house!!!

I just don't get it!

And I've also noticed that fashion does go in stages.

Short skirts are back in again like they were back in the sixties.

Although you can't actually call some of them skirts.

A strip of cotton more like.

If my daughter thinks she's going out looking like that when she's older....

I sound like my father.

Talking of which I remember finding an old Starsky and Hutch style 1970's leather jacket in his wardrobe once.

He's a bit like me you see.

Or rather, I'm a bit like him.

A hoarder!

I always remember asking him why he just didn't just throw it out because in the eighties he would have looked ridiculous in it.

Imagine that, wearing a cool looking 1970's leather jacket in an era when we all thought shell suits looked good?!

"One day son, it will come back round again!"

Yeah, and so will polio and no one will be wanting that either!

But he's right.

Fashion has come back round again.

And it would actually be a really cool looking leather jacket to wear today, and how cool that it is an *original* 1970 one and not some fake 1970's look-a-like one

Except, of course, he can never actually wear it.

And why?

Because he's now seventy and no longer looks like David Soul but instead looks more like a geriatric Huggy Bear in it.

I don't really know why I didn't get swept along with all the eighties fashion trends.

My mates did.

And I went through all the *other* various stages of teenage hood with them.

Listening to The Sex Pistols
At least until my parents told me to '*turn that rubbish off!*'

And I actually did find it pretty rubbish if the truth be known.

I was the only wannabe punk, teenager that actually dressed quite conservatively and listened to Barry Manilow when no one else was in earshot.

Well, my mother used to listen to Barry Manilow and you know when you hear a song over and over you eventually come to like it.

'*A weekend in New England*' always brought a tear to my eye.

In fact my wife took me to Vegas for my fortieth and I was secretly hoping she had booked us tickets to see him.

Of course I couldn't actually tell her this.

And of course she hadn't.

Wearing skinny jeans
And I mean so skinny it was as if they were sprayed on.

God knows how I actually managed to produce two kids later in life they were that tight.

Had you stared at my groin through my jeans you'd have thought my testicles were wearing earings.

I had a mid-life crisis moment in TK Maxx just recently and bought some skinny jeans.

I think it was because that manufactured boy band that seems to somehow be taking the world by storm at the moment, One Direction or One D as my eight year old daughter calls them, and she'd know as she forms the upper end of their fan base, all wear them and something inside me, you know that inner sense that we all have that tells you '*you look bloody ridiculous*' popped out for a cup of tea at the same time that I stood in front of the mirror staring at myself in them and I must have somehow said '*yeah, these actually look quite good for a forty year old*'.

And then of course I got them home, tried them on again and showed my wife.

And let's just say her reaction wasn't quite as complimentary as I thought it would be.

So I binned them.

Red Doctor Martin boots
Well, my mates got the boots actually and I ended up with Doctor Martin *shoes*.

In black.

As my mum thought they looked much nicer and would also last longer.

Plus I could wear them for school.

Good old mum -- always thinking practically!

Underage smoking
That was a definitive *must do* if you wanted to look *really* hard.

And cool.

Again, I tried it.

Once.

And when I say *'tried'* it, I mean... I listened to the advice of one of my mates who we all looked up to as he was a *professional* smoker and he told me to *'suck on it so the smoke goes into your mouth and then just breath it in just like you're breathing'*.

So I did.

In fact I followed his advice a little *too* closely.

Do you remember that scene from The Exorcist?

You know the one when the possessed girl throws up literally *everywhere*.

Well that was me.

For about FIVE hours.

In fact I threw up so much my mother thought I had been poisoned.

"How does anyone EVER take a second drag?"

"You just have to keep doing it mate," said in a very broad northern accent.

And he was right… you really do have to put a lot of time and work into smoking.

Going to house parties
And being rowdy.

We were never at the stage of smashing things up, which looking back now I'm very grateful for.

I remember being about eighteen and somehow one of our mates, you know the mate that you don't regularly hang round with but every now and again they pop up and actually you have a really good night out with them?

Well that one turned up at the pub one night to say he'd been invited to this bird's (yeah, sorry not my words) eighteenth birthday bash out in the middle of nowhere, so always up for a good party we headed over.

Now this bird's (sorry, just wanted to set the scene properly) dad was well known back where we lived for selling arcade machines for a living and oh my God, he must have sold a lot.

Long gravel driveway.

Electric gates.

Fountain in the middle of an in and out driveway.

Ferrari!

The biggest house I'd ever seen.

In fact it was so big, I nipped off to the loo at one point and didn't find my mates again for half an hour.

They had a swimming pool.

A games room -- full of arcade machines, naturally.

It was a teenager's paradise.

And it was also rammed full of bloody teenagers.

Note to self....

NEVER!

EVER!

Allow my kids to have a house party round at our house.

Now I don't really know what her parents must have been thinking.

Clearly up to this point in their lives they'd never actually met other teenagers.

Especially not the kind of teenagers that turn up en mass and all carrying bottles of cheap cider with them.

There were teenagers EVERYWHERE!

Teenagers in corridors.

Teenagers in bedrooms.

Teenagers in the garden.

Teenagers fighting.

Teenagers snogging.

Teenagers wrecking things.

And incredibly the parents were still in the house.

Hyperventilating!

As two hundred drunken, rowdy thugs went about systematically smashing up anything and everything they could.

It was like a biblical plague of locusts destroying everything in its path.

I mean they did a proper *'rock star in a hotel room'* job on the whole place.

The only thing they didn't have in that house was a panic room and I bet they've got one now.

Although I can't imagine they ever let their daughter have another party there.

In the end the police were called and the house was cleared and as the mom and dad sat crying hysterically in the kitchen, me and my mates cleaned up.

And I don't mean we robbed the place.

Oh no!

We actually cleaned up for them.

Real rebellious eh?!

And they didn't even thank us for it.

How rude of them!

And so began the start of our *'Big Time'* house parties.

Where I grew up we had a guy known as 'The Sausage King'.

Now I appreciate the title might concoct some kind of sordid mental image and you'd be forgiven for thinking along those lines... but it wasn't that kind of *'sausage.'*

He actually *sold* sausages for a living.

At least *he* didn't.

The massive work force that he employed did.

At least I assume it was his company.

He did carry himself a little like that movie character 'Arthur' played by Dudley More, who had loads of money but no actual responsibility.

Or sense.

And he was a real legend in our town.

Not because he had loads of money.

More because of how he spent it.

Think of a northern Hugh Hefner crossed with Elton John in his most extravagant period and that's kind of the image that I think best sums him up.

He'd turn up at our local pub dressed like some town crier and instead of a bell he'd carry an ice bucket overflowing with bottles of Veuve Clicquot under one arm and a gaggle of glammed up (and drunk) teenage girls under the other.

Now it wasn't exactly some classy pub that we used to frequent, oh no.

In fact it was far from it.

I quite expect to see it featured on *'Britain's Toughest Pubs'*, so as you can imagine he didn't quite blend in all that well and he wasn't exactly a shy and retiring character either.

But then again I don't actually think it was his intention to blend in.

Rather... show off!

All the regular hard nuts used to leave him alone.

In fact they actually used to suck up to him as they either thought:

1. He might give them money.

Or

2. He probably has people tougher than them on his payroll.

So once a year the Sausage King would throw his annual summer party and it was a *'get an invite, turn up and then pay on the door'* affair.

So….

My mate got us an invite.

And a car load of us turned up to his house.

Now this house was big.

Probably not as big as the other one but big enough.

AND

Apparently it was his *party* house.

His other house….

Apparently….

Was so bloody big it actually had a runway in the garden for his private plane to land and take off on.

So as my mates headed over to the main entrance of his party house I concocted a cunning plan.

The house was huge, as were the gardens, and the winding fence that contain said gardens didn't look all that high.

And sure enough it wasn't.

The only thing is, as you can probably imagine, a house of this calibre needed to have a good security system.

And it did.

A very good one.

In the form of brambles, nettles and loads of other spiky, clothes ripping, flesh tearing plants and bushes.

Not to be put off though, and to save me from having to pay the twenty pound entrance fee, I bravely fought my way through -- like a knight, battling through the thorn bushes to rescue Sleeping Beauty if you like.

Just without a sword, armour or any bloody body (or face) protection for that matter.

And yes, I was wearing my smart, bird (sorry) pulling clothes.

Some of the bushes were VERY thick and consequently almost impassable, so the only way I could get past them was by doing a kind of weird army crawl where I caterpillared my body forward using my four limbs trying desperately not to let any part of my clothing touch the floor -- or rather, the mud.

Impossible.

I felt like Bear Grylls -- only a really hopeless, pathetic, tight arsed version.

It took me about ten minutes to traverse my way through this jungle I was in.

I, by the end of it, really did look like I'd been dragged through a hedge backwards.

And I had.

I was filthy.

My hair was a mess.

I'd torn my shirt.

But it was worth it as I'd saved myself twenty pounds.

While my mates had all coughed up their entry fee like a bunch of suckers, I'd beaten the system.

Take that '*The Man!*'

Only trouble now was I had to make it from my hiding place at the edge of his tree lined forest to the party -- which in my favour was also going on outside.

It was the summer after all.

BUT!

As his garden was so big, none of the guests were anywhere near the forest's edge.

And, they'd no doubt all see me sneak out.

Plus, looking the way I now did, there was no way I could just casually stroll out, hands in my pockets and whistling a merry tune without any of his security spotting me.

And booting me out.

So I waited.

And I waited.

Hidden.

Hoping for that perfect moment when I could make my move.

Head out unnoticed and join the party.

But it didn't come.

It wouldn't have been so bad had I walked out of the forest with a girl but oh no, I had to be on my own, and what would that have looked like.

Like I'd been in the forest *with* a girl, murdered her and buried her still warm corpse.

Oh my GOD!

I started to panic.

And then did something really brave.

Or stupid.

I just strolled out.

Now luckily for me the Sausage King didn't have security that night.

Or any night so I later learnt.

But he did have about two hundred guests who now all stared, open mouthed at me as I casually made my way up the garden, throwing polite nods at people as I passed them all while trying my hardest to look as *'normal'* as I could but instead resembling a modern day Stig of the Dump.

And I wasn't even drunk!

"Where the hell did you get to?"

"Yeah, well check this out you bunch of losers, I snook in through the woods. Saved myself twenty pounds! Yeah… paying's for idiots!"

I remember saying this with a real smug grin on my now, mud covered face.

My mates all stared at me in disbelief.

So it turns out it was actually free to get in.

God knows where we had all got *'twenty pounds'* from.

Needless to say I went home alone *again* that night.

So, during my rebellious stage I thought it would be really cool, and a bit *'way out'* even, to get a tarantula.

Except no one actually told me that they live for about eight years.

Plus, my parents didn't want anything to do with it.

Especially as I had bought it without actually asking their permission first.

So I was on my own -- with this great big, bloody hairy spider the size of your hand that lived for at least eight years and I was currently eighteen.

That meant that I would NEVER be able to settle down with anyone and get a place of our own as my parents wouldn't look after it and I couldn't just release it into the wild.

Never really thought that one through either did I?!

Plus, you couldn't actually do anything with it as you couldn't pick the bloody thing up as every time I so much as peeled back the corner of its lid, it would rear up at me and start hissing.

And it was supposed to be the friendliest breed on the planet!

I guess someone had forgotten to tell *it* that.

And as you can imagine, inviting a girl back to your bedroom so that you can *'listen to mix tapes together'* doesn't really work when there's a bloody great poisonous spider staring at us both from the corner of the room!

And it used to escape.

Oh my God, there's nothing that will get your heart pumping faster than walking into your bedroom one night and finding it's not in its tank.

Then having to search through all the nooks and crannies in your bedroom with a torch and the end of a broom handle re-enacting that scene from 'Alien' when the mouth sucker thing had laid its egg in the scientist's body and done a runner!

God knows how it would escape though as I always thought I had it all secure.

In the end I'd have to gaffer tape the lid shut while resting a pile of house bricks on top, just in case

And it never moved.

In fact it didn't actually do *anything*.

It really was the biggest waste of time and money when I look back.

I remember peeling back its lid on one occasion to throw in a few crickets and wondered why, for the first time ever, it didn't rear up at me.

Turns out it had been dead a week.

So we bought my son a lizard.

A Bearded Dragon in fact.

One of the tamest of all the lizards, apparently.

And it is.

In fact, it's just downright dopey.

And he called it 'Boris Johnson'.

Apparently it looks like Boris Johnson but I don't think my son actually has a clue what Boris Johnson looks like as his lizard certainly doesn't have a mop of blond hair on top of its bald head.

"No, dad you have to turn him upside down!"

"Who, Boris Johnson?"

"Yes. No. The lizard. If you turn him upside down *then* he looks like Boris Johnson!"

"Do you even know who Boris Johnson is?"

But apparently he has a white under head (which I just call, his chin) so if you turn him upside down, which I think might actually be boarding on animal cruelty, he does look *a little bit* like Boris Johnson.

Let's just hope it doesn't last as long as that bloody spider did.

Or even as long as the *real* Boris Johnson, for that matter.

Chapter Eleven

In It To Win It

The wife's entry

Apparently we've won the lottery!

Not one of those fake Microsoft Lottery's either, where your e-mail address has somehow been chosen at random, even though you never entered their draw or you don't actually have that e-mail address or they're unable to confirm what your e-mail address actually is as the one they've sent it to isn't showing which means they've just sent a random e-mail to thousands of people in the hope that someone sends them the taxes so they can then release the millions.

I do feel sorry for people that get caught by that scam.

Or so I told my husband.

You see, I received an e-mail from eBay recently informing me that they were about to suspend my trading account as one of my sellers had lodged a complaint against me.

Needless to say I was devastated!

It all looked official.

There was even a message from the seller to eBay lodging their complaint.

I did think it was strange though as I didn't actually remember advertising a 'selection of unlocked mobile phones' for sale.

In fact the only thing that I ever do sell is the kids old clothes which they've since grown out of, but being the good kind of Samaritan that I am and certainly not wanting to upset someone that's kind enough to bid on one of my items, I clicked on the link and signed in using my user name and password.

Strangely though it didn't seem to allow me to do much more.

So I tried again

And again.

But all with no such luck.

'System must be down' I thought, so I just closed my browser and planned to try again later.

"YOU'VE DONE WHAT?!"

"Well it looked official."

"Of course it did. That's the whole point of a scam! They're hardly going to bodge together a crap looking e-mail in the hope that the receiver is simply half asleep, or drunk, and won't notice!"

"Oh!"

Luckily my husband managed to change all my passwords and so far our bank accounts haven't been wiped out.

Plus, what were they planning to do with my eBay account anyway?

Sell things for me?

It's not like I actually gave them my credit card number and security code or anything.

So anyway that's me banned from eBay for the distant future, which actually suits me fine as he can now spend hours ironing and then photographing kids clothes, copying them onto the pc, uploading them to eBay, along with a description that is going to catch someone's attention -- only then to have them sell for just ninety nine pence.

It's unbelievable.

If I wanted to buy a second hand pair of boy's football boots on eBay for example, I'd end up paying more for them than I could get them brand new from Sports Direct.

But when I try to sell anything....

Ninety nine pence!

Everything that I stick up there just sells for ninety nine pence.

And, as you probably know, ninety nine pence is the maximum starting price to ensure you don't pay a listing fee, so in actual fact I'm only actually getting *one* bid.

One bid!

I put my daughter's bike on Ebay recently.

Plus her pink bike horn (only because I couldn't work out how to get it off) and also her bike helmet that she had grown out of.

Second hand, excellent condition... the usual stuff for a bike that's only really been ridden when the sun shines, which as you'll know isn't very often in this country.

And it went for two pound fifty.

TWO POUND FIFTY!

FOR A PRACTICALLY BRAND NEW BIKE!

AND HELMET!

AND HORN!

In fact I seem to remember the horn actually cost four ninety nine when we bought it to go on the bike.

So the lucky bidder actually got a half price horn and a free bike and cycle helmet.

And to top it all the dad that came to collect it gave me three pounds and told me to 'keep the change.'

If I had just waited on his table and he paid me a fifty bloody pence tip I'd have thrown it back at him.

Fifty pence!

What am I going to do with that?

Put it towards her new bike because that will *really* help.

So anyway… we've won the official lottery.

I know this because my husband shouted it up the stairs.

He does the lottery online each week.

He's pretty self-disciplined with it.

He just does the one line on the Euromillions each Friday.

"Well I don't smoke or drink so what's the odd two pounds here and there?"

Exactly, because that's not going to mount up much over the fifteen years is it now?

If it goes up to a hundred million, which it often does, he may buy two lines.

I've never really got my head around this mentality.

So twenty million isn't worth a four pound investment for two lines but one hundred million is?

I know, I know… you can buy so little with twenty million these days.

To be honest, I actually think it's a waste.

I mean have you ever met anyone that's won millions on the lottery?

People win all the time apparently and we've both travelled around a bit but neither of us personally knows anyone that's ever won big.

And I mean *really* big.

My husband thinks it's a conspiracy.

That the machine has to be so sophisticated that it's quite possible it could know in advance as to which numbers have been picked by the general public throughout the week and then purposefully not draw those numbers out on the night.

This would of course encourage the poor unsuspecting general public to spend even more money on it the following week as the jackpot increases and consequently earns the organisers even more profit.

And yet he still does it.

And he buys a second line every time the jackpot goes up as well.

And *he* thinks it's a conspiracy.

Says it all really.

"How much?" I shout down.

"I don't know."

"Well find out."

It's pretty much the same conversation we have every time he gets one of those e-mails.

You see it's happened several times before.

He gets a message telling him *'You have some exciting news about your lottery ticket'* but he refuses to click on the link and find out how much he's won because that way he can go for the whole weekend thinking he's a millionaire until I finally have enough, click on the bloody link myself and discover that he's won £2.80 for four correct numbers.

What a swizz.

He did actually get four numbers once plus one of the bonus star things and won forty eight pounds.

Forty eight pounds!

He was only two numbers away from getting all of them and all he won was forty eight pounds.

So while he sits there at the computer I make my appearance.

"Oh, Hi honey...."

And before he knows what's happening I've spun him out of the way in his revolving office chair, and clicked on the link myself.

"What the...."

"Yep, you've made eighty pence -- again!"

"What did you do that for?"

"Really? You have to ask? How many eighty 'P's do you think you have to win to become a millionaire then eh?!"

"A lot!" shouts my daughter from the kitchen.

"I really don't have the time."

And as he sits there thinking *what the hell just happened* I stroll casually back upstairs to finish putting on my make-up and getting on with real life once more.

Chapter Twelve

The Terrible Truth

The husband's entry

"Guess what Mum… Dad said the 'F' word, right in front of me!"

BLOODY SNITCH!

But it was true -- I had.

A simple, slip of the tongue.

Easily done.

But in my defence, I didn't actually realise my son was in earshot.

It was one of those moments when you're out with your mates (and the boy) and for some reason you momentarily forget that you're in your forties and somehow seem to slip back to your teenage years when it's all cool to swear and be loutish and the kids are somewhere else playing, not sure where, but just not mithering us, and out it comes.

It was one of *those* moments.

Plus, and in my defence (not that I really have a defence) I hadn't actually instigated the original conversation that resulted in my little *'slip up.'*

My little *'misdemeanour.'*

I'd just verbalised my thoughts or rather, my appreciation of the story I was listening to in the only way a man knows how….

By swearing!

The expletives were of course in full flow anyway, as they usually were at this stage of our regular little Sunday lunchtime get-togethers and no sooner had the word passed over my lips, the small crowd of bodies that were currently hiding my son, parted like Moses parting the waves of the Red Sea and there, with his hand once again held firmly out like Oliver Twist wanting more (money -- as usual) but instead of the usual pleading look he instead wore a huge, smug *'I've got you now old man'* grin instead, was my kid ready to extort his way through a whole weekend of treats, presents, Ipad and Playstation time along with all the usual banned (because it's brain numbing -- and more for me than them) kids TV.

And all at my expense -- just so he wouldn't tell his mum!

What IS the deal with kids TV anyway?

When I was a kid all we had in the way of children's entertainment was Tizwas with the great Chris Tarrant, or for the posher kids, Saturday Morning Swap Shop with Noel Edmonds, and then, only until lunchtime, which is when the TV companies naturally assumed that your father would have gotten his lazy arse out of bed and usher you off out to play and as far away from him as possible.

I walked in on the kids watching some computer generated television rubbish recently and had to walk out again five minutes later as there was SO much happening on the screen, so fast and all at the same time that I thought I was about to have a fit.

That or a stroke.

But so it was.

The damage done.

And me, held over his blackmailing little barrel.

At least until there was something even bigger to blackmail me about.

Just wait till you turn eighteen son.

PAYBACK!

And who says kids are innocent?!

But that was the price I had to pay for corrupting him with my, oh so colourful language.

His little ten year old virgin ears suddenly no longer all that innocent.

Years of having to explain my side of the story to his Grandparents, over and over again, each time he brings it up at family get-togethers.

Which of course he will.

It's not that kids are rubbish at keeping secrets!

They're just a damn sight cleverer than we give them credit for.

And as I momentarily looked deep into his eyes... he knew it!

And to be honest, I'm not even that big on swearing.

I help out at some of my own kids afterschool clubs so I really do have to mind my 'P's & 'Q's

And what are 'P's & 'Q's anyway?

I mean, everyone swears from time to time.

The odd little slip of the tongue.

In some cases I actually think a little colourful language here and there can sometimes help improve a story.

Set the scene better.

Raise the narrative a little.

And in my defence (have I used that line already?) comedians do it all the time and generally get bigger laughs as a result.

So when the circumstances dictate, I don't have a massive problem with the occasional bit of profanity.

Just not in front of my son.

And not because he's never heard it before.

Or because as a result of my bad parenting he'll some day be recounting this incident on a psychiatrists chair.

No.

Because I knew it was going to cost me dearly.

And so did he!

I remember the first time I ever heard my father swear.

I was about seventeen and had to catch the train to college and as the train station was much too far away to walk and he couldn't be bothered to drive me, he offered to lend me his bike.

And a rain coat for when it rained.

Thanks dad!

Now as you've probably gathered by now my father is a bit of a hoarder.

And a real tight arse.

Plus he's getting on a bit as well.

So when he said he'd lend me his bike, I half expected it to be a Penny Farthing.

Luckily for me it wasn't because he would have still expected me to ride it.

He brought me a car once.

It was an Austin Maxi (remember those -- if not, Google it and have a laugh!)

And it was brown -- I think they only came in brown.

Hideous things they were!

I don't think he actually brought it for me.

I think he *actually* brought it to do up, sell on and make a nicer littler earner from.

But not only was it a bloody awful looking car, this one in particular was a real old knacker.

And a right old rust bucket.

And my father, being quite the unskilled mechanic that he was (and still is) thought *'doing it up'* simply meant *washing it* and so that given, as it still drove like a bag of spanners despite it being a *little* bit cleaner, naturally nobody wanted it.

And I can't blame them.

So in turn he tried to fob it off on me.

But not give it to me.

Oh no.

Sell it to me!

And for *'a good price'* as well.

And so when I told him I'd rather walk... it didn't go down too well.

Mainly because I think I was his last hope at getting any money back before cutting his losses and taking it to the scrap heap.

Clearly that's where I get *my* business acumen from as well.

So because his bike was so old, and because most of the other bikes at the train station were actually *of* the current decade (and I mean they had inflatable tyres, brakes and saddles that you could actually sit on because they hadn't perished away), I didn't bother to lock it up all that securely.

In fact I didn't actually bother to lock it up at all as I figured any would be bike thief would be more inclined to leave the bike and steal the lock as it was worth more.

And so naturally it got nicked.

And naturally I had to tell him.

And naturally he really wasn't happy.

And he swore!

And it was a real shock.

Hearing your father utter those words that until now only your mates or the rough necks at school would say, really took me by surprise.

So in a strange and perhaps not *quite* the same way, I sort of knew how my son *could* be feeling.

However....

As much of a shock as it was to hear my old man swear, nothing came as more of a shock than the time the old coffin dodger lent me a porno movie.

"Here you go son, have a gander at this when you're mum's next out! There's a guy in it with a todger the size of a baby's arm!"

So blasé!

Those words just... rolled off your tongue Dad.

Effortlessly!

'You do of course realise that I'm not one of your factory working mates, and we're not down the Working Man's Club now don't you?!' -- I thought.

Apparently not.

And apparently my father was lending me a porno which I for one, certainly couldn't recall ever making any reference to requesting.

Especially from him.

And that's not because as a fifteen year old, testosterone fuelled teenager I wasn't into that kind of thing.

No!

I just wasn't into borrowing them off my Dad!

But I secretly think he lent it to me because he thought there was a chance I might be gay.

And I'm not joking either.

He even asked me once.

"Son, are you gay?... Err, because if you are then that's okay of course!"

Thanks Dad.

And the fact that you even had to add that last bit in means that actually, in your eyes, it's far from okay!

You see Dad was a real man's man.

And big into football.

Saturday mornings were for watching 'World of Sport with Dickie Davies' and NOT for spending time with your kids.

And then Sunday's were for playing footie in the *'Working Man's Club --*
Sunday League' and seeing how many of the opposition you could send
to A&E.

NOT for spending time with your kids.

And Dad was a real legend when it came to *'Sunday League Working*
Man's Club' football.

He could knobble the hardiest of players with just one, over
enthusiastic, studs up, sliding tackle.

And as such, I felt it only right that, due to much peer pressure and
because of the fact that I wanted my old man to be proud of me -- and
because as a kid back in the seventies, football was really all there was
to do, I too signed up with a local kids Sunday league football team.

And I say *'signed up'*....

It was the local housing estate team and to be honest I *was* actually
quite proud to be representing my housing estate.

In fact I was actually really surprised (gob smacked to be fair) that they
had picked me for the team as, let's say, I wasn't a natural footballer.

In fact I was rubbish.

Kicking a ball really didn't come easy to me.

And the only reason I did get picked was because no one else bothered
to turn up for the trials.

And they were desperate!

But in my defence, they *were* actually a relatively decent team....

That was until I joined.

Sunday after Sunday I'd turn up to play and Sunday after Sunday we'd
get thrashed.

On one occasion we lost twenty two nil.

Yes *twenty* two nil

I remember telling my father we lost that day and he said *'not to worry son, two nil's not too bad a defeat.'*

He spat his pint of mild everywhere when I proceeded to correct his auditory mistake.

So he eventually dragged himself away from his *'Working Man's Club pre-roast dinner drink'* to watch me play one cold, wet, Sunday morning.

And not because he wanted to impart his years of footballing wisdom upon me in order to make me a better player.

Or even to show me some moral support.

But mainly, I think, because even he thought that we literally couldn't be THAT bad and he just had to see it with his own eyes.

I remember it well because we were playing the worst team in the league that day so were all confident of at least one less defeat during the season.

And I also remember it because I scored a goal.

And, well... when I say *'scored a goal'*....

The ball was passed beautifully to me by one of my seven team mates as I ran up the centre of the pitch.

Yeah... the other four hadn't bothered to turn up again.

Pretty standard!

It bounced just a few feet in front of me.

The goalie was momentarily caught off his line as he half expected my team mate to try for a shot.

Even I could have told him there was no chance of that as our approach to playing football was a little more *'please don't pass the ball to me'* and when you were unfortunate enough to have the ball roll anywhere near to you, you just booted it as far away from you as you could.

In any direction!

So it was an open goal.

I sprinted towards the ball.

Even I was thinking *'what the hell am I thinking?'*

But my father was watching this match.

And I wanted to make him proud.

The crowd was screaming.

"GO ON SON! SHOOT! SCORE!"

I could hear them.

All other sounds were now drowned out.

This was going to be the very first goal we'd scored all season.

And I was about to score it.

It could be our first ever non-goal less defeat.

I saw the ball in front of me.

The other team's player now sprinted for it as well.

But I was closer to it.

And I had time.

Valuable time.

Don't rush this.

Focus your mind.

Clear it of all negative thought.

Even the sound of the crowd was now closed off to me.

I was in a state of focused consciousness (I don't even know what that really means!).

It was like that end scene in the original Karate Kid movie when Daniel Larusso goes into that weird stance thing that's supposed to represent a bird or something and time seems to halt and everything just goes really quiet for a brief second before he lands that final kick that wins him the fight.

It was a bit like that -- just without the bandana wrapped around my head.

I closed the gap.

The ball right in front of me.

Mid sprint I lined up the shot.

The coach was screaming 'SHOOT, SHOOT, SHOOT!'

Fingers were crossed.

Mine included.

The other player was now only inches away -- closing fast.

The goalie desperately trying to scramble back to his goal line.

With Daniel at the forefront of all my thoughts now I threw out my kicking leg as hard as I could....

And missed!

And then slipped over.

And the other team's player whipped in front of me, got the ball and bloody well scored.

And as rib splitting laughter instantly replaced the previous roar of a hopeful crowd, all that I could focus on were those four words that left our team coach's mouth as he shouted his message of encouragement to me....

"Son... you're a WANKER!"

So fifteen nil to them!

But at least we did get some recognition in the end....

The title for being *'The WORST team in the league.'*

So I think that based on my dismal performance on a football pitch and the fact that he, his three brothers and his father were all great footballers, the possibility of me being gay was the *only* justifiable explanation for being so crap at the beautiful game.

"You're son's pretty shite when it comes to kicking a ball mate!"

"Yeah, that's 'cos he's a fagot!"

"Oh right!"

Like that would silence the doubters.

And at the same time be far more socially acceptable than him having to admit to all his footballing cronies that *'Goal Hanging Henry's'* son wasn't actually all that good at football.

So I honestly believe that my old man lent me his stereotypical, heterosexual porno movie to see how I'd react.

And I'm happy to say I *did* watch it.

Just once.

Mainly out of curiosity as to the baby armed, over endowed gentleman my father had previously made reference to.

And to be honest, I think I was more shocked as to the quality of the acting than anything else.

But of course, me being me, even *that* viewing didn't go smoothly.

Back in the eighties VHS cassette players weren't all that cheap.

We did own one.

But it was only one.

Unlike today when the flashing lights in a teenagers bedroom closely resemble airplane cockpits because they're so crammed full of the latest technology that they could spend their remaining years never having to venture out into the real world and somehow still manage to outlive their parents.

Just!

Our VHS player was in the lounge.

A room often inhabited by all the family.

And as I'd been informed to *'not tell your mother I have this though'* I had to pick my viewing evening very carefully.

You know… so I could watch it discreetly.

So having been informed that my parents were off out the following Saturday, I got busy on the phone.

And invited pretty much ALL my mates round to watch it.

Well it was a momentous occasion as a teenager.

Much like your first kiss or getting served your first pint in the local pub when you clearly weren't old enough to be served but if you just stuck a cigarette behind your ear that might fool the old barmaid enough to actually serve you.

Or of course because she just didn't actually give a toss how old you were.

Plus, where I grew up she'd have probably been your first kiss as well.

So I was going to watch a porno.

It was a moment that had to be shared.

Plus it was going to make me really popular with all the cool kids at school.

I couldn't wait for the playground chatter on Monday morning.

So 8.00pm and the parents went out leaving me all home alone.

8.01pm and me, plus twenty of my mates, a bottle of Diamond White in each of our sweaty little palms all pile round a tiny, CRT TV with a twinkle in our pervy little eyes.

I hit play on the VCR (as ours didn't come with a remote), and took my seat amongst them.

And we all drew a deep breath as the video sprang into life.

And then let it out again.

"What the hell's this shit?"

Playing out on the screen in front of us now could once have quite possibly been some quality seventies Swedish porn movie, except the one we were now watching had either been watched so many times it was worn out.

Or it had just been copied too many times.

Regardless of the actual reason, all that it now resembled was that scene in Poltergeist when the little girl sits in front of a TV with nothing but that black and white 'fuzz' all over the screen.

"No… If you stare hard, and squint a bit, you can make something out!"

Well that was it… twenty, fifteen year old tearaways all leaning forwards, squinting at a black and white flickering TV screen as hard as they could through one eye.

That's how desperate we all were to get a glimpse of boobs.

So after ten minutes of 'is that boobs… oh no it's someone's head' they had all but given up and my credibility as to my claim of being the new Hugh Hefner was in some considerable doubt.

So, disappointed and somewhat deflated, we left to go and terrorise some old people as was in keeping with the weekend activities of fifteen year boys at the time.

Only joking!

Instead we just walked around the streets talking about which one of us would be the first to get lucky (get a snog -- and hopefully from a real girl) or better still, own a Lamborghini Countach.

I returned home later that night, thankfully before my parents, as in my haste to leave at the same time as all my mates I had forgotten to remove the tape from the VCR.

And unfortunately for me, my father had also forgotten to remove the little tab that prevents anyone from recording over what was previously on it.

And as I reached down to eject the tape my heart skipped a beat as I suddenly see that sight that no fifteen year old kid that has been given the responsibility of looking after his Dad's porno film ever wants to see in his life….

The TIMER RECORD light flashing away.

So not only does my father now think I couldn't possibly have watched his porno movie as I'm unable to accurately describe any part of it to him.

But he also thinks I taped *'Larry Grayson's Generation Game'* over it.

And as Larry Grayson was the campest guy on TV at the time....

There was no other explanation for it....

I had to be gay!

Chapter Thirteen

It's Christmas Time

The husband's entry

So we've put our Christmas tree up.

And it's the middle of November.

I know it's very *'Bah Humbug'* of me but I believe there should be a law passed that states you're only allowed to get in the Christmas spirit from the 1st December -- at least!

Personally I'd prefer, the week *before* Christmas, but I know that's expecting too much even for an old scrooge like me.

We visited that great big corner shop in London once -- Harrods... and it was September, I think.

Possible even August....

Anyway, whichever month it was it was a damn sight earlier than it should have been (by law) and they had a Christmas section and the whole of the section, which I seem to remember was pretty much the whole of the basement floor, was geared up towards Christmas.

Christmas decorations.

Christmas cards.

Even Christmas carols blasting out of the speakers.

And God knows when they actually opened this Christmas section of their store (it could be all year round knowing Harrods as let's face it, this used to be the store that sold lions in the pet department) but I do remember asking one of the highly strung workers if there's a chance they'd be on suicide watch by October and in their typical *'we're working for Harrods and therefore are so much more superior than your average shop assistants and possibly even YOU'* kind of way, just simply smiled and lied just, as I can only imagine, he had done fifty times already that day.

I do love Harrods shop assistants though….

I think that's where all the ex-Concorde cabin crew ended up!

Anyway, I couldn't get out of there quick enough… and I wasn't even working there.

Plus, there's something seriously wrong with hearing Christmas songs when it's not December.

It probably doesn't help when there are no *new* Christmas songs.

For the past forty odd years I've listened to the same old bloody Christmas songs over and over again.

Occasionally some has-been, washed up rapper tries to launch his own unique version of a gangster style, shoot em' up Christmas melody, but it generally always flops quicker than one of Cliff Richard's latest incarnations.

According to Google, Slade earn over half a million pounds each Christmas just from '*Merry Christmas Everybody*' alone!

No wonder all these boy bands with their very short life spans are desperately trying to get in on the Christmas number one act.

And who can blame them?!

East 17 hasn't done too badly and all they *literally* did was add Christmas bells to their song '*Stay Another Day*' and it got to the number one spot on Christmas day, thus making it… a Christmas number one.

And I'm all for it if nothing other than to give us all something new and original to look forward to that isn't simply a re-edited version of *'Do they know it's Bloody Christmas'* for the hundredth time.

All they do is change the odd word, modernise the singers and then expect us to go out and part with our hard earned cash once more.

And I would if it wasn't for the fact that it sounds EXACTLY the same as the last three I bought, none of which actually sound as good as the original one, and all of them containing Bono wearing what looks like a pair of those night time driving glasses that the elderly wear.

Was that part of the agreement that he has to be in *every single* version for the rest of time?

And did he come up with *that* line and then somehow managed to copyright it?

God knows, but when you only actually know *two* of the singers in it this time round, you know it's time to simply let the latest version pass quietly by and if I really did want to listen to it again (which I don't), then I can just pull out the 1984 version -- which I do still have and in my opinion, is far superior.

And why don't all those multi-millionaire pop stars just save us all the pain of having to endure another version of the same record for yet another cause that doesn't really benefit anyone either here *or* in the country they're trying to save for that matter as we all know, thanks to the papers, that the corrupt governments that run those country keep it all for themselves anyway, and instead cough up just a small percentage of what they're worth and surely that would amount to more than they'll actually raise from trying to convince the poor do-gooder general public to put our hands in our pockets yet again.

And I wouldn't mind were it not for the fact that if you've ever watched the making of Band Aid 1984 you'll see that most of them arrived at the recording studio in limos and several got flown back into the UK on Concorde.

And we all know how much good that thing did for the Carbon Footprint.

When Frank Skinner re-launched that 1996 England European championship song 'Three Lions' again for the 1998 World Cup, we all went -- 'REALLY?!'

Just changing the players' names to reflect the new team does not constitute a good enough reason to buy it a second time round -- especially as we all know, it won't make the blindest bit of difference to us actually winning.

Could J K Rowley re-write Harry Potter by just changing the names of a few of the characters?

So anyway, back to the Christmas tree and the kids are just brilliant.

They know to start planting the seed (excuse the pun) at least a week before.

"Can we put the Christmas tree up next weekend?"

"No!"

"Can we put the Christmas tree up next weekend?"

"No!"

"Can we put the Christmas tree up next weekend?"

"No!"

"Can we put the Christmas tree up next weekend?"

"No!"

And so it goes on all week, each day drawing closer to the bloody weekend.

And then of course the weekend arrives and as is typical with the British weather at this time of year... rain puts paid to our (my) plans of going out for the day which I was hoping to do to take their mind off putting up the Christmas tree and of course we end up stuck around the house.

With nothing to do.

No stimulating or productive indoor plans.

Other than putting up a Christmas tree.

Four weeks too early!

And so it continues, like a badly scratched record.

"Can we put the Christmas tree up?"

"No!"

"Can we put the Christmas tree up?"

"No!"

And then they sucker punch me....

"Why not?"

"Because it's the middle of November and I have rules and I'm in charge and when you both own your own houses then you can put the bloody Christmas tree up in January for all I care but until then what I say goes - - understand?!"

My wife glares at me.

And so we put the Christmas tree up and everyone's happy.

At least they should have been.

But of course, as with anything in our household it's never quite that simple.

Our *'Christmas Tree Erection Experience'* begins with me heading up the loft.

All I have to actually aid me during this stage of our adventure is a wobbly old step ladder that doesn't quite reach the loft hatch, and a knackered old head torch -- strapped to my head like a 1970's miner -- which is the era that I think the head torch actually came from.

Thanks Dad!

And after each ritualistic and death defying loft escape I always make a mental note to buy a new step ladder *and* a new head torch... or even just bite the bullet and get a light installed -- but of course I never do.

To be honest I do actually like rooting through all the loft junk.

It's like an Aladdin's Cave up there.

I feel like Indiana Jones raiding that lost ark.

So I climb the rickety step ladder as my wife holds them steady and the kids' camcord the whole event in the hope of making themselves two hundred and fifty pounds.

I fling the loft hatch back, switch on the head torch and hoist myself up and into the black abyss of the damp and dingy roof space.

Then begins the standard search for all the Christmas related stuff we have up there which is always buried underneath all the other junk that somehow manages to get thrown up throughout the proceeding twelve months and I, once again, think to myself... *'I really need to sort this loft out.'*

Perhaps I don't actually need to keep *every* box from *everything* we (I) have ever bought, after all.

By the time I do actually get round to putting it on eBay *'in its original box and packaging',* the bloody thing is knackered anyway!

In fact I've found boxes for things that even I forgot I once owned, still up there!

It's like being born again as I descend back through the loft hatch opening and into society as any recollection of thoughts that I may have had from my previous life (up the loft) always get wiped out on my 're-birth.'

So I find *four* Christmas trees because I always say *'we're not going to buy a real tree as it's a waste of money and an artificial one will last forever and just think how much that will save us!'* and yet somehow end up buying a new and more realistic artificial tree each year instead -- none of which look anything like a real tree... so of course I might as well have just bought a real tree.

And so begins the military style operation of getting all the stuff down without squashing the kids, killing the wife or just letting it drop as I precariously balance my whole body weight on two small and very narrow beams.

To make life just a little easier for myself I concoct a rope and pulley system that allows the heavier stuff to be gently lowered down and while I remain in the comfort and safety of my dark, spider ridden loft, the kids fight it out between themselves as to who's going to swing on it.

And eventually we (and I mean 'I') get it all out, make a mental note that I need to tidy up the loft and buy a new torch or even get lighting installed and begin the re-birth process.

And of course there's no one there to *'receive me'* or even steady the ladder now as they're all downstairs and far too concerned with tearing all the gaffer tape off the boxes to remember me.

By the time I arrive in the lounge it looks like we've been hit with a blizzard.

Snow (from the snow covered Christmas tree) literally covers everything.

Sofas.

Carpets.

Kids.

Wife.

And I just have to take a big deep breath and grab the vacuum cleaner.

"What are you doing?"

"If we clean as we go then there'll be less mess!"

She cuts me a look!

And then comes out with the words that I always dread on such occasions....

"We need Christmas Songs!"

The kids drop everything and tear out of the lounge.

All we hear from our little Antarctic hide-away is....

A scream.

A thump.

A shout of pain.

Something getting knocked over.

A cat rapidly scurrying away.

And then my son reappears breathing heavily and clutching the Ipad in his grubby little hands.

"What happened?"

"Nothing!"

His sister appears at the doorway -- a clump of his hair in her fist.

And so while my son spends the next fifteen minutes searching for a Christmas song that he likes (or even knows), which of course is never going to happen as 'Guns n Roses', as far as I am aware, never actually wrote any Christmas songs, I set about trying desperately to untwist snow covered wire *'branches'* in a futile attempt to get them to just remotely resemble something that looks like a tree as my wife frantically tries to untangle the Christmas tree lights -- again.

And then gives up.

Which is why we have eight sets of Christmas tree lights.

All of which need untangling.

"Persevere, cos we're not buying a ninth set!"

She does and with a little (loads) of help from me and the two kids acting as vertical support poles so we can wrap the bits we have untangled round them -- all while the boy *still* searches for a Christmas song he likes!

An hour, more vacuuming and several beers later and our perseverance finally pays off as we have two completely entwined kids, both desperately in need of the toilet and a start and end point to the lights.

I take charge.

"Start winding your child round the left hand side of the tree and I'll wind my child round the right!"

Referring to the lights of course.

And so the tree starts to slowly take shape.

A little more vacuuming and it's tinsel time.

I (foolishly) let my daughter have free reign with this -- I mean there's no way letting my eight year old loose with a whole box of tinsel could go any way other than perfect now is there?!

So twenty minutes later and you'd be forgiven for thinking a heard of wild buffalo, each draped in Christmas tinsel had stampeded their way through our lounge, round the tree several times before making good their escape.

I crack open another beer.

Vacuum up the mess.

Next stage -- baubles.

Which of course have to be colour matched -- red and gold, and spaced evenly so they are symmetrical on all sides starting with the large ones at the bottom and slowly graduating to the smaller ones at the top.

At least that's how it should be done.

Ours....

Well, it looks like my daughter simply threw the box of baubles at the tree from the other side of the lounge.

I finally snatch the Ipad off my son and put on the latest version of 'Band Aid'.

Final stage is of course all those other things that we're all conned in to buying by our kids.

Pine cones -- 'really... I have to pay money for something I could just pick up off the lawn?'

"Bah Humbug Dad!"

And of course all the things the kids have ever made during their years at pre-school, infant school and now junior school.

And it's never ending.

You can't actually see the tree anymore.

Not an ounce of green in sight.

And there's still snow EVERYWHERE!!!

Is it *actually* snowing in here?!

And then my daughter launches the bombshell.

"Whose turn is it to put the angel on top this year?"

We all stop dead in our tracks.

I throw my wife a concerned look.

She returns it.

Discreetly shrugs her shoulders.

We then endure those five stages of grief from our kids.

Denial
"You did it last year"
"No I didn't!"
"Yes you did!"

For five minutes

Anger
"I hate you -- it's my turn!"
"I hate you more!"

Bargaining
"If you let me do it this year, you can do it next year!"
"Well if you let *me* do it this year I'll let YOU do it next year!"

Depression
Which is just simply both of them in tears and my wife and I desperately

148

trying to console them while also desperately trying to work out a solution that doesn't simply involve me bloody doing it to shut them both up.

Acceptance
"Right, let's toss a coin for it!"
"Okay, fine... I'm heads!
"No, I'm heads!"

And so begins the *'five stages of grief'* once again....

So in the end our Ipad addicted son actually has a brainwave.

"I'll look back over the family videos (on the Ipad) and see who did it last year."

Now this would have actually been a pretty good idea were it not for the fact that for some bizarre reason 'FAMILY LIFE 2013' isn't actually on the Ipad.

However 'FAMILY LIFE 2012' is, so he commences that while we all stand in silence and watch.

Five minutes and another beer later and I have to ask "Have you found it yet?"

"I'm only at March!"

And so all silent praise that my wife and I had in that moment for our brilliant little future hostage negotiator son is instantly lost!

"Fast forward it you muppet!"

He does.

"Well!"

"Hang on!"

"What do you mean 'hang on', where are you at already?"

"I think it's November".

"Well is it or not?"

"Yes, it's definitely November as the cat has antlers on."

"So... who put the fairy on the tree?"

"I don't know."

"What do you mean you don't know?!"

"It's not on there! -- I'll check two thousand and eleven!"

"NO!" -- The simultaneous shout from both myself and my wife rings out throughout the lounge.

And so in the end the only acceptable solution is....

My daughter puts the fairy on the tree, and I give my son a fiver!

We step back to admire this thing that we have created.

Some might call it a Christmas tree but not me.

Yes, I know... Bah Humbug!

My wife proudly slides the tree into position -- near to the plug sockets.

"Hang on... let me get the camcorder!" my daughter announces as I realise that once again we've forgotten to video who put the fairy on top and of course it's too late to take it off and do it again as that would constitute her doing it twice in a row and I can't afford another fiver.

"Okay... ready?" My wife enthusiastically asks.

My daughter hits 'record'.

Nods.

The little red light flicks on at the front of the camcorder.

And with a huge smile on her face my wife plugs in the lights so that Christmas in our household can commence!

Nothing happens!

Not even a flicker from a solitary bulb.

She unplugs them.

Tries the other socket.

Still nothing!

So as tradition once again dictates we find ourselves back in Argos buying our tenth set of Christmas tree lights and….

Our fifth bloody artificial Christmas tree that looks just a little bit more like a REAL tree!

Chapter Fourteen

You've Been Framed

The wife's entry

So my husband's taken our son windsurfing and the weather forecast says it's *'seventeen mile per hour'* winds.

'So they must be pretty good at it then?' I hear you ask.

No!

In fact... quite the opposite.

In fact... it's only my husband's third go and my son's very first lesson.

To be honest, I simply put it down to being another one of those daft mid-lifer adrenaline activity things if you ask me.

I half expected him to take it up with his other mid-lifer's but to be honest as my son's the only one daft enough to join him, he has little choice really but to share the experience with him.

No doubt my husband hasn't told my son the lake water is going to be cold either.

We went to Centreparcs a few years ago and my husband told our two kids that the water in the plunge pool was really warm.

So in typical *'trust whatever your father says'* fashion and before I had chance to tell them that *'it's your father, of course he's lying'*, both kids are dive bombing it right into the freezing cold water to the shocked gasps of disbelief from all the other swimmers in the nice warm (and packed) outdoor heated swimming pool.

Well they both flew out of there like a couple of Polaris missiles at the same time as the whole swimming pool spins round to see my husband killing himself laughing.

"They didn't even test the water!" he roars. "I'd have at least dipped a toe in first!"

Needless to say, *'Father of the Year'* award will not be going to him this year.

Or any other year come to think of it.

So my daughter and I tag along for the ride and to offer them both some moral support.

And for the laugh.

Now prior to this he's had two private lessons and has somehow managed to pass his level one windsurfing exam which basically means someone in their infinite wisdom thinks it's safe to let him go out on his own on a lake with this bloody great contraption that I assume must be worth quite a bit of money and do so unsupervised.

"Honey… what's the worst that could happen?"

"You could drown!"

"Look, they wouldn't have signed me off if they didn't think I'd be safe on it."

Really?

By the lack of other people on the lake today (because they're not stupid enough to go windsurfing in seventeen mile per hour winds and in freezing cold weather conditions) it would seem to me that they're just grateful to be able to take his money to pay their bills.

So he waddles out of the changing shack in his wetsuit and I burst out laughing.

"What?"

There are lumps and bulges that I didn't even know he had protruding out of it at all angles.

"It's a bit tight."

"It's supposed to be."

"And are you supposed to be able to breathe in it as well?"

At which point he dons his buoyancy aid and waddles over towards his board and sail.

A confused look embraces him and I see him waddle back over to one of the staff members.

They exchange words and he waddles back over to the board with a concerned look on his face.

"Everything alright?"

"Fine."

Moments later he's on the jetty, windsurfer all rigged up and him all set to cast off.

I ready the camcorder.

Might as well earn two hundred and fifty pounds while I'm here.

He steps tentatively onto the board with one foot.

Then the other.

Wobbles.

And falls in.

My daughter awards him with a huge standing ovation.

"He wasn't supposed to do that you know."

"Wasn't he?"

"No, the idea is you balance on the board."

She sits back down.

In the meantime my son is having his private lesson on the shore as it's far too windy for him to actually be out on the lake.

I personally think it's far too windy for my husband as well but after he smugly informed us all that he's never fallen in which, and I quote *'is probably because he has really good balance'* and not forgetting the fact, as I point out, he's only actually had two other goes, I'm here just to watch him eat that humble pie.

So he's back up on the board again.

And then back in the water again.

"He's not very good is he mummy."

"No sweetheart, he's not."

I keep recording.

"ARE YOU KIDDING ME!"

"Everything alright honey?"

He cuts me a look.

Then slips back into the freezing cold water again.

It's like a scene from a cartoon.

Now it wouldn't be so bad but he hasn't actually left the jetty yet.

"RIGHT! That's it!"

He detaches the sail.

Throws it on the bank.

Picks up the board under his arm.

Storms back over to us and throws it down.

"It's the wrong board."

"Oh. Okay…."

"Don't!"

He storms off looking for a staff member.

"I don't think Daddy's very happy mummy."

"Never mind honey… mummy is."

He re-appears next to us.

Apparently once you finish your training you can no longer use a training board as:

One -- they're great huge things that you can't possibly fall off unless you only had one leg or were just blind and missed your footing.

And two -- they need them for the trainees.

So instead, they put you on a standard board which, apparently if you're any good, should be fine.

Well he's not.

In fact he's far from good.

Or fine.

And from behind the storage shed two staff members appear carrying a huge great windsurfing board between them, lug it down to the jetty, attach his sail to it and then leave the rest to him.

"Shouldn't he be on the other board?" I enquire as they pass.

"Yeah, he *should*."

I smile to myself and press record again.

So he paddles himself out to the middle of the lake this time and in his defence manages to stand up.

He reaches down, grabs hold of the line and very slowly and methodically lifts the sail out of the water taking hold of the centre mast with both hands as he's been taught.

So far so good.

He carefully takes hold of the sail's control bar with his nearest hand, the brake hand so I understand, and brings the sail into its balanced position.

He very carefully re-positions his feet so as to keep everything perfectly balanced.

"Daddy's doing good."

"Keep watching."

He lets go of the centre mast with his other hand (the accelerator hand) and cautiously places it into position on the control bar.

He takes a deep breath.

Pulls the sail in.

And the seventeen mile per hour wind hits it full on.

Well all I can say is what follows next simply resembles one of those Jackass style sketches where the poor devil that has been chosen to undertake the current challenge has no bloody clue what the hell is happening to them, or how to control it, and simply hangs on for dear life.

We both watch, open mouthed as he careers full speed towards the fast approaching, solid looking, embankment.

Even the two staff members take a few steps forwards to get a better look.

His backside flails around unnervingly as he desperately tries to counter balance the sail -- incorrectly.

Forwards.

Backwards.

Forwards.

Backwards.

"Is daddy dancing mummy?"

"I don't think so honey."

Meanwhile I zoom in to see, quite clearly now, him screaming out words that I can't possibly print here.

Luckily as he was now moving so fast and I felt sure he'd broken the sound barrier, it protected my innocent little eight year olds ears.

Or... he just simply couldn't get the words out.

"If he just lets go of the sail he'll be fine," muses one of the staff members.

He doesn't, and the next thing I know the windsurfer's gently floating back towards us all on its own and he's drowning in the reeds.

"I'll get the speed boat," says the same staff member.

So needless to say by husband is now banned from said water sports school as they decided that it's far cheaper for them to lose him as a student than increase their insurance to cover all the potential damage that he's likely to cause from windsurfing there.

And after watching his father show him *'how it should be done'*, my son has now decided it wasn't really for him after all!

Chapter Fifteen

Happy Holidays

The husband's entry

Do you know what I find amusing?

People that live on an entirely different planet to the rest of us.

And I don't *literally* mean *'people that live on an entirely different planet to the rest of us'* of course.

I'm not referring to UFO's here or indeed trying to convince you as to the existence of little green men with a sense of humour-- despite *'Mars Attacks'* being quite a humorous movie.

And rest assured that this isn't the stage where I turn all Jehovah's Witness on you -- engage you in a completely different topic of conversation in the previous chapters and then try to skilfully convert you over to my way of thinking without you even realising.

That's the next chapter!

And what did Jehovah actually witness anyway that's worth knocking on my door all dressed up at eight AM on a Sunday morning for?

No, I am of course metaphorically speaking and actually mean 'people that clearly *do* live on the same planet as us -- but are just mad!'

Just like all those loons who claim to have been abducted by people that actually do live on other planets!

Those are the kinds of people I'm talking about.

The mad ones.

They're the ones that are *'on another planet'*.

And there's LOADS of them out there.

All out there mixing in society.

With us *'normal'* folk!

My wife (girlfriend at the time) decided to hire a personal fitness instructor to get her in shape for our upcoming beach holiday and although I personally didn't think she needed to... at the same time I also thought there was nothing wrong with her tightening up those saddle bags a bit.

So I was a little surprised when my wife (girlfriend at the time) returned home a little earlier than I had originally anticipated and then proceeded to informed me that the fitness instructor who she was about to hand over her hard earned cash to in return for being shown how to get a six pack, was stuffing her fat face with a KFC when she walked in... so she simply walked back out again.

What was that fitness instructor thinking?

And it was a fat face as well apparently which also didn't help her cause!

But it actually turned out that she did have a six pack -- of full fat coke... in the fridge.

I mean what is the deal with overweight fitness instructors anyway?

And this isn't the bit where I get all politically incorrect on you.

But I have to say if I *was* to employ the services of a health and fitness guru to help me get fit and healthy, I would be more inclined to believe that they actually knew what they were doing if they, themselves, looked a little less like Jabba the Hut and more like Arnold Schwarzenegger.

And that's just the women!

Confidence in your service person is key, so I believe.

I mean, would you employ the professional services of someone to teach you how to drive a car that kept crashing.

And how far do you take it?

Would you be happy watching a circus show where the entertainers didn't so much perform, but more... told you what they would have done had they been able to do it?

Practice what you preach is what I was always told!

But then I was also told to *do as I say and not as I do* which is just totally confusing.

Especially when you're a small child.

And yes, I know they *can* teach me how to drive, just like my wife's fat fitness instructor *could* tell her how to get a six pack, but wouldn't you much rather be taught by someone that *does* practice what they preach on this important occasion?

Someone that could perhaps run round the track with you instead of standing on the side line, full fat, creamy latee in hand, shouting *'Come on! Push yourself! Feel the burn!'*

'You'll feel the bloody burn when I've finished!'

The even more ironic thing is... she was apparently sipping on a bottle of Lucozade.

Why?

Had her jaws finally *'hit the wall'* from all that chewing?

Needed a bit more energy to help her get through that last handful of chips?

Would you take marital advice from a divorced marriage guidance councillor?

Hire a security guard that's got a criminal record for theft?

Do you see what I'm getting at?

And I also have to ask the question *'are you seriously on the same planet as us'* when those **TWENTY YEAR OLD** *'celebrities'* put out yet another, updated autobiography all about how they (but really, Simon Cowell) made it (manufactured them).

You're twenty!

You haven't even lived yet!

But it's not the celebrity I'm actually questioning here.

Good for them!

It's the people that buy their half written life story.

Or Cliff Richard for putting out yet another Christmas calendar of his wrinkly old self!

What is he thinking?

Or anyone that actually buys it for that matter.

Stop encouraging him!

Are there still people alive that have even heard of Cliff or remotely even know who he is?

You know you're getting older when the youth of today have no idea who John Wayne is.

Or Marilyn Monroe.

Or James Dean.

Or Bruce Lee.

And I particularly love those wannabes that consist mainly of people who concoct the most amazing stories about things that they haven't actually done.

Like rescuing people during 9/11 when they weren't even there.

The fake heroes.

All of it made up!

A little bit like me writing this book then?!

NO!

I'm only joking!

Ninety Five percent true!

Or those people that put their whole life on social media but can't actually engage you in conversation.

Or just those people that put their whole life on social media, FULL STOP!

What's the deal with that?

Who even cares that you've just finished your sixth coffee and it's only lunchtime.

Or it's 3am and you can't sleep.

Do you know what I'd do?

Instead of reaching for your laptop....

Close your bloody eyes!

And no wonder you can't sleep if you've had six coffees throughout the day.

I had someone once, a female (of course) that would send me the most confident and flirtatious e-mails to the point where I thought I was going to have to say something to her or my wife might think there was actually something going on.

I soon realised that I (or my very supportive and understanding -- thanks honey... wife) had nothing to worry about when the woman in question was unable to hold a *conversation* with me, let alone hold eye contact.

And not because she actually had a thing for me and that's why she couldn't engage me in eye contact.

No.

But because she had no interpersonal skills.

None at all.

I even thought I had got the wrong person she was that different in the flesh.

A real Jeckle and Hyde!

Or maybe perhaps just schizophrenic!

Or mad!

Or people that pay to go to weight watchers, get suicidal when they don't lose any weight and say '*I can't understand it, as I hardly eat a thing!*'

Well let me help you there....

You clearly do!

We had a friend once.

A female friend.

I don't really know why her sex is that important but I thought I'd help set the scene a little better for you.

She did the Weight Watchers thing every Monday morning and every Monday lunchtime my wife would get a depressed phone call from her telling her that she'd not lost anything (except the twenty pounds it cost her to turn up).

Now me, I'm a little less sympathetic, but my wife would say all the right things and console her -- which I actually think was part of the problem.

The other part of the problem was the fact that every Friday she'd buy up the complete fast food aisle of the local supermarket and cram it all down her throat by Sunday evening.

And then visit Weight Watchers on Monday morning.

And then get depressed.

And then eat more to make herself feel better.

Why do people that get a ticket for parking on double yellow lines get angry about it?

Do you know what I'd do?

....

So my wife, who in her defence, probably doesn't really need to lose any weight but as it turns out she thinks she does... either that or we seem to have bought all the mirrors in our house from the same place that the fun fair gets theirs from, so I endure a month of having to go through the same automated replies like *'of course your bum doesn't look big in that shoelace of a bikini you're desperately trying to cram it into'* and being constantly snapped at because she's LITERALY starving.

I half expect *'Hunger Relief International'* to beat the door down any moment and cram some food down her throat.

And what IS the right course of action for any man when their wife (or girlfriend) asks THAT most terrifying and marriage / relationship destroying of questions?

"Do I look good / fat / slim / busty / ugly in this?"

Or worse….

"Do I look as good / slim / pretty as her?" referring to the airbrushed catwalk model in the magazine she's casually flicking through.

I mean clearly judging by the fact that there are so many fat women wearing leggings outdoors we're all simply terrified of the consequences if we say what we're really thinking.

I tried it once.

My wife innocently asked me THAT question.

"Honey, do I look okay in this dress?"

And I thought I'd reply with….

"No my sweet, you look like you've just stepped out of a Marks & Spencer catalogue!"

Admittedly after reading that line back now it makes total sense as to why there were all those empty boxes of rat poison in the recycling bin the following week and all my meals throughout that same time period tasted a little funny.

So help us out ladies -- we're not that bright!

When you ask us what we think of what you're wearing.

Or how you look.

You also need to give us a little clue as to what you're expecting us to say.

What you'd like to actually hear.

Maybe hold some possible answer cards up even.

Would that be too much to ask?

Even those poor fools that bum out on the hundred pound 'Who Wants To Be A Millionaire' question could have asked the audience at least.

And when you say 'and now be honest', we need to know that that's *not* what you really mean and you in turn need to realise that if you actually say those very words, being the one dimensional males that we are, the part of our brain that governs rational thinking thinks it's been let of the hook and pops out to get some milk and we just say the first thing that comes into our heads which is normally exactly what we are thinking and of course the EXACT opposite of what you want us to say and we then end up regretting our reply for the rest of the day.

And our lives.

And to make it even worse... don't even know what it was that we did or said that got you so upset!

So having spent a whole day searching for a cheap holiday that we could afford on Ceefax....

Remember that?

Like an antiquated World Wide Web.

However did we cope before Google?

Even when we booked it, we didn't actually have a clue where we were going to end up as we (and I say 'we'... I mean 'I') refused to pay the extra that confirmed where we *would* end up.

That was the beauty of Ceefax....

"It's like an electronic lucky dip!" -- so I told my wife (girlfriend at the time).

But she doesn't buy it.

And we end up at some cheap resort in the Dominican Republic.

But at least it's the Caribbean, right?!

So anyway, it takes us a few days to get acquainted with the place.

Get settled in if you like.

And we're on an all inclusive package as well.

Oh yes... only the best for us!

We (I) are such skin flints that we (I) aren't prepared to pay the extra to choose our own, half decent, resort... but I'm prepared to pay a little extra to go all inclusive and if paying a little extra to go all inclusive means we get a free bar -- who gives a shit anyway!

And the only reason we (I) paid extra to upgrade to all inclusive is because I genuinely believed that I could eat and drink more food and alcohol than the amount I paid for the upgrade, thereby making it extremely cost effective and possibly even a right bargain (and of course a challenge!).

And after the first few days of gorging myself to the point of vomiting, my wife (girlfriend at the time) can't stand it any longer and consequently decides it's time to go on an excursion.

Which I think is just a ploy to get me away from all the free stuff as I was into my *'fat'* trunks already and it was only day three!

And mainly because she thinks I may actually eat and drink myself to death if we don't.

On that note, I have a sliding scale of swimming trunks (or rather swimming shorts now I've turned middle aged as cramming my family jewels into a piece of cloth so small and tight you would easily be able to tell if I was Jewish or not probably isn't the most befitting for a middle aged man, with middle aged spread -- I mean, after all, I'm not Spanish now am I, who, based on my last holiday to Spain, just don't seem to care about that kind of thing and the tighter, smaller and more revealing the better -- regardless of age, size... or just plain decency!), which consist initially of 'the arrival pair'.

The *arrival pair* is the pair that I can *normally* get into when I'm living my normal, *all inclusive free* life and although they are far from 'skinny fit', at least I can still breathe when I wear them.

Followed within a few (short) days time by the slightly comfier pair for when all inclusive is still a novelty.

Followed not long after that by the pair with the elasticated waistband.

Followed by the pair with the tie string and the waistband that was once elasticated but even the elastic gave up the ghost and snapped on me after one fateful lunchtime binge (I thought I'd suddenly developed a hernia when that happened -- imagine my relief when I realised it wasn't my stomach lining snapping), and so now it's just a saggy waistline with a draw string -- which seems to work fine for me.

And God Forbid, we stay any longer than ten days and then it's basically a potato sack with leg holes cut in, all held up with a frayed rope.

And after *that* I'm just not allowed outside in case Green Peace turns up and tries to throw me back in the sea.

So we (she) books us both on a simple tour of the island that leaves at six the following morning.

And to really get us in the holiday mood I suggest we have a few drinks and a little something to eat!

☺

So we pull up a stool at the free bar and as I sample the local (free) beer, my wife decides to try just one of the local (free) cocktails.

Just the one of course as we have an early start.

And then we get chatting to another couple at the bar.

And the conversation starts flowing.

And so do the cocktails

Two.

Three.

Four cocktails later and they're going down my *'girlfriend at the time's'* neck very nicely.

And it would be very rude of us to go so soon as we've only just met this nice couple so we (she) has another.

And another.

And another.

And before we know it, it's about one in the morning and I decide it's probably time to call it a night as I know my wife (girlfriend at the time) can sometimes... not always of course honey, but now and again... struggle with the odd hangover in the morning after having a tiny bit too much to drink the night before.

And in her defence (and my total amazement), she does actually appear to be fine as she refuses to go all while still somehow managing to engage our new best friends in the most witty of contemporary banter.

So the five AM alarm call rudely disturbs my much needed slumber and I jump out of bed like Usain Bolt off the starting blocks, wondering how on earth I got into bed, grab the phone and do my best to pretend to the very sweet Spanish sounding receptionist that I'm not your stereotypical British pisshead and that I am capable of stringing a sentence together whilst having drunk their free bar dry only several hours earlier.

But I needn't have bothered as by the time I finally managed to coherently say the words 'I'm up, I'm up!" so they don't sound like I'm telling her to 'shut up!' she's already making her next wake up call.

So I stager in to the en suite, take care of what comes naturally, and decide it's probably best I brush my teeth in order to....

One -- take away the taste of whatever the hell it was I was drinking last night.

And two -- to reduce the chances of getting anyone I happen to talk to within the next few hours, pissed from the pure stench of my breath.

And as I lean over the sink using the basin as a support I realise my beautiful girlfriend (at the time) is still laying in bed comatosed and we need to be in reception in thirty minutes.

So I shout over gently words of light encouragement.

"GET YOUR ARSE OUT OF BED AS WE NEED TO BE DOWNSTAIRS IN THIRTY MINUTES!"

And she sits bolt upright like Frankenstein's monster having just had 50,000 volts fired into him.

Relieved that she's not dead I continue brushing, all the while keeping a sneaky little *'corner of my eye style'* watch on her to ensure that it wasn't just a knee jerk reaction and that she's not going to simply slam her head back down on the pillow and fall back to sleep again.

Or better still... remain fast asleep but in this upright position.

And I wouldn't have put it past her.

Thankfully I observe her throw aside her bed clothes.

Swing her legs off the bed and onto the floor.

And then stand up.

And I say 'stand up'....

I actually watch, in gobsmacked disbelieve, toothbrush now just hanging out of my open mouth, as my girlfriend (at the time) attempts to take a step forwards, completely loses her balance, slams face first into the bedside wall, slides all along the full length of the same wall in a sort of stumbling, desperately trying to catch her balance at the same time, kind of way, literally landing full force into the wall at the other end of the bedroom, and then sliding slowly down into a still very clearly drunken unconscious heap.

'Oh my God she's dead!' I think, as I spit out the toothbrush and sprint over to her fully expecting to have to give her CPR and silently praying that I didn't, because I didn't actually know how to do it.

Something about pushing down on her boobs and breathing heavily in to her mouth.

She'd be used to that with me!

I lift her head and see her eyes roll back.

I panic and do the only thing that I can think of doing in this moment of high intense pressure....

I slap her across the face.

Her eyes flick open.

THANK GOD!

And then instead of gently carrying her back to the bed and laying her softly down and calling down to reception to tell them that my girlfriend (at the time) is not very well and can you please let the tour guide know we're going to have to miss the trip....

I simply say....

"Sort your bloody self out as we've paid for this bloody trip so we're bloody well going!"

Yeah... I will admit now that on reflection I could have perhaps been a little more sympathetic.

So, as she's completely out of it and as I've made up both of our minds that we're still going and as there's not much time, I simply dress her in the same clothes she had on last night as I really don't have the energy to choose anything from the wardrobe that can or can't go together and as it takes *her* about an hour to decide what to wear each morning, what the hell kind of hope have I got, so as she was happy in what she had on last night I simply figure *'that'll do'*.

And I then realise she's slept in her make-up and it's now smeared all over her face and I can't let her go out looking like that -- even though our photo album would just be the best God damn photo album in the world if I did, but even I can't be that cruel.

So I decide that I have to do the unthinkable.

Clean her up.

So I'm now standing in the bathroom, bottles of clear liquid in my hands, trying to work out which one takes off make-up and which one makes it worse.

I give up, grab some toilet roll, soak it under the tap and race back over to her and start scrubbing.

And five minutes later all I've actually managed to do is make her look like a demonic clown.

'What the hell does she put on her face that water and a shit load of scrubbing won't shift?!'

She'd have actually looked better if I'd have just left things as they were.

And all while she just lays there like a rag doll.

But I don't care as time's fast running out, so I hoist her up and, doing our best interpretation of a three legged race (well it's either that or simply stroll in to the hotel's reception area with her slung over my shoulder as I greet everyone with a casual *'good morning'* as if this is simply the most normal thing in the world), somehow manage to frog march her down several flights of stairs and into reception where, to my horror, everyone's waiting for us, including the couple we met the night before.

"Is your girlfriend okay?"

I could tell by the look of horror on their faces they too didn't think I'd done all that good a job on the make-up front.

"Something she ate!" -- I reply with a nervous smile hoping they don't think I've actually killed her and am now doing my best to re-enact that movie 'A Weekend at Bernie's' so no one suspects a thing.

Good old universally recognised (and appreciated) throw away alternative and politically correct response for THAT question when asked by people you're still desperately trying to impress!

'Something she ate!'

So we board the coach with its fixed and un-opening windows and the tour guide announces the one thing that I really did not want her to announce at that exact moment and in thirty degrees heat at six AM in the morning with my girlfriend (at the time) still pissed and nauseous….

"The air conditioning's knackered!"

But not to worry as it's only an hour to the meeting point.

Yeah… an hour of hell, as my girlfriend (at the time) slips in and out of consciousness.

And how do I know that she is actually slipping in and out of consciousness, as I have my back turned so far away from her at this point I might as well having been sitting on the old man's lap in the row opposite me?

I know, because of the noise she's constantly making each time she passes out and her forehead THUDS, once again, onto the coach's bloody fixed and un-opening, air conditionless window like some sadistic, parcel shelf nodding dog that's lost the will to live and is either trying to head butt itself to death or smash the glass and throw itself under the wheels of the coach.

It gets so bad that I begin to think she'll give herself brain damage so decide to do the only think that I can think of given the circumstances I find myself in (and not having a gun handy!) and decide that the only way I can possibly stop her constantly fading in and out of consciousness is to simply inflict pain upon her.

So I pinch her.

As hard as I can.

And she sits bolt upright -- Frankenstein's monster all over again.

"Where are we?" she questions. A look of surprise slapped right across her Crusty the Clown face.

I don't even have time to answer before she's head butting that window again.

How many bloody cocktails did she sink?

I pinch her again.

She sits bolt upright again.

I can see her brain desperately trying to process everything and not being able to.

She stares vacantly into my eyes.

"What are you doing?"

"Saving your bloody life!"

The old woman in the row behind pops a concerned head between our headrests having clearly been witness to this strange lover's sadistic ritual taking place between us where my girlfriend constantly bangs her head against the glass and I pinch her as hard as I can.

"Is everything okay?"

I throw back my best attempt at a sympathetic *'thank you for your concern but mind your own bloody business and please don't draw any further attention to this whole messed up scenario as we may just about get away with not being given the title 'those two Piss-Heads' when being referred to back at the resort later'* face.

"Something she ate."

She nods a knowing nod.

That's it -- we've been branded!

So what seems like an eternity later and we finally arrive at our meeting point.

Thank God!

Anything to get off this bloody coach.

And just when I thought it couldn't get any worse I catch sight of our new mode of transport.

An opened topped, re-converted, all terrain, former missile carrier... with a beer fridge!

And it was so bloody big you had to literally climb a ladder to get in it.

Somehow she managed.

"Is everyone sitting comfortably?"

The crowd throw back a huge cheer.

"Then let's head to our first stop... a cheese making factory... now who wants some alcohol!"

Are you kidding me!

A cheese *making* factory.

Just the smell of Cheese alone makes you want to throw up and we're going to be visiting the place that bloody well makes it?

In thirty degrees heat?

It's going to STINK!

My heart rate rises and my mouth goes dry as the co-driver throws back cans of warm, cheap beer.

I grab one of them -- SOD IT!

So we arrive and my girlfriend (at the time) chooses to sit this stop out which was the most sensible thing she'd done so far, as after about twenty of the longest minutes of my life, most of us walk back out of there -- green.

"Next stop, a chocolate making plant!"

Okay, at least chocolate smells quite nice -- a whole lot better than cheese at least.

I turn to my girlfriend to get the thumbs up but she's hanging over the side of the missile launcher having thrown up so much she's now just fast asleep.

Each bump and her head thumps along in time and I've just got no energy to hoist her back in the cab so she stays like that till we arrive at the next location.

As we pull up she wakes.

Sits up.

"Chocolate plant… you joining us?"

She nods and we both eventually catch up with the back end of the tour as the tour guide expertly informs everyone how these trees that we can all see in front of us contain the cocoa beans that they use to make chocolate and how they carefully pick those beans and then grind them down into a fine powder and then they take the powder that they then get from this process and mix it with something and blah, blah, blah.

And none of it matters anyway as no one's actually listening to him.

No.

Instead they're all watching in disbelief as my girlfriend, bent over, skimpy little knickers and rear end on full display to everyone, retches up her guts in the corner of his chocolate tree field… before all turning their attention to me.

I simply smile nervously and say….

"Something she ate!"

Well eventually I have to come clean as even I can't simply bullshit my way through the whole of this tour, and as we've already been branded now, it doesn't matter to me anymore anyway.

At the lunch stop one of the locals approaches and asks in his best Spanglish….

"Your girlfriend… she is not well?"

No shit Sherlock!

"Give her this… get her to sip it."

He hands me a plastic cup with some green looking liquid in it.

"Look Pal, I appreciate you trying to help and all but what they may have neglected to tell you is that she ain't keeping *anything* down!"

He simply smiles and says.

"Trust me!"

He goes to walk off.

Stops...

"Oh, and the cocktails... nasty! All made with local rum!"

So I thank him and take the green stuff over to the spot on the ground where she's currently sleeping like a homeless dog, knowing full well what the outcome of getting her to drink this will be and at the same time a part of me is thinking 'is this just one big wind up? Are they videoing this for their new hit TV show 'Look what else we can get those stupid, British pissheads to drink! -- they'll drink ANYTHING!'

And with just the slightest bit of envy toward everyone tucking in to a hearty looking meal as I'm now starving, I think that I probably do need to stay with my still pissed girlfriend and burp her like a new born if we (I) are to claw back any ounce of respect and decency we may have once had and recover from this.

Well, I somehow convince her not to tip it away and in fairness to her (and why wouldn't she have reason to trust me -- just wait till she sees all those photo's I've been taking of her) she follows my instructions to the letter.

And, God only knows what was in that shit, but within ten minutes of her finishing whatever it was, she was not only as right as rain but was also tucking into her plateful of braised donkey like she'd been stuck on a desert island for the past three weeks.

And not only did she make me promise NEVER to tell anyone about her little misdemeanour -- and, it IS a true story, I promise you....

She also promised me that she'd never touch another rum laden cocktail again for the rest of her life.

Especially if it was made with local rum.

And especially if that local rum was SEVENTY percent proof -- like Dominican Republic rum!

Chapter Sixteen

Committing Treason

The husband's entry

I do love a good day out.

I was very fortunate to have lots of them in my last job, and not because I was always skiving off but because my job involved me working at shows and exhibitions.

Which was essentially just a good skive!

With a bit of work thrown in.

I have friends that are pilots and whereas those of us that aren't pilots naturally assume it must be a *great* job, jetting off all over the world and seeing all those exotic countries -- *and* with all those lovely cabin crew.

But speaking to my pilot friends, they hate it.

The constant jet lag.

Lack of sleep.

Hours and hours of just sitting.

And then to top it all, not actually getting to see anything of where they've landed because before you know it they're back on the plane for the journey home.

And so it turns out that just like every job we think must be pretty cool because we don't do it, after a while the novelty soon wears off.

A bit like going on holiday and within the first few days of doing bugger all you think it's heaven and you could do it forever and then after about ten days of doing nothing but gorging yourself to the point where you're fast becoming a prime candidate for type two diabetes… a small part of you is actually looking forward to getting back home again.

And Broccoli!

And then of course you arrive back to the cold, wet, miserable British weather and simply think….

'I wish I was back there!'

And so you book your next holiday on your phone on the drive home from the airport and simply proceed to wish the year (and your life) away, only to go through the exact same thing all over again next year.

My wife suffers from post holiday depression so badly that she actually books our next holiday while we're *still* on holiday.

She gets depressed about coming back home while we're *still* on holiday.

Last year the resort we booked turned out to be dire.

In fact *dire* was probably being too kind.

We were conned in to booking it by one of those estate agent type brochures.

You know the one… where they use those special cameras that make the neighbour's house seem like it's miles away from the one you're looking at and then when you turn up for your viewing it turns out that if you and your neighbour took a shower at the same time (in your respective bathrooms) with your windows open you could actually pass each other the soap.

And you wouldn't even need to stretch.

That's it *'estate agent photographer's'* -- YOU'VE made my book!

What's the point of flouncing up the photo's of the house you're trying to sell only to then have to deal with some really pissed off potential buyers when they turn up to see it.

And I know estate agents think we're all pretty stupid and that we really do believe them when they say that *the ex drug den, urine soaked, flea pit has 'potential'*... but really?

And I get *why* they do it, but it's like advertising a Porsche on Auto Trader and then when you turn up for the test drive it turns out to be a Prius.

No one's going to buy it so what's the point?!

But you can't do that with a holiday.

You just have to trust the brochure and if it's not as it seems when you arrive then you're generally stuck there until it ends.

So anyway, we ended up at this hell hole of a resort and we were feeling really out of place because we didn't have any tattoos and despite being there a few hours we weren't paralytic.

You know it's not going to be good when the coach pulls up outside and even the kids refuse to get off.

And to make it worse we booked it with friends but Virgin had cocked up and thought that our friends had booked into the system twice and so deleted the second booking only to later discover (and I mean literally a week before we were due to fly) that it might just be possible there's more than one family in the whole world with the surname 'Smith'!

And of course it turned out that it *wasn't* a double booking.

It was an oversight on Virgin's part.

And it also turned out that instead of just checking, which you'd *think* would be the first logical and obvious step, the little YTS kid that is in control of people's lives... and just to be clear, our annual holiday IS a huge deal Mr Branson... that little YTS kid just deleted them off the system.

Just like that.

But, and in Virgin's defence, they did correct the problem.

They found them an alternate flight *and* as the resort we were all planning to stay out was now full, offered them an upgrade to a MUCH nicer resort.

And let's face it, anywhere would have been nicer than where *we* ended up.

Even ten days in Afghanistan!

And I'm sure that the YTS kid thought that that was the end of it -- a happy family, but oh how wrong he was as it was the WORST thing that could have come out of it because our two families were now staying at separate ends of the country.

And so began a campaign by our respective wives to bring the Virgin empire to its knees, or at least get them to stick us back together again, which consisted mainly of calling them up and asking politely, then shouting, then crying, then screaming, then asking politely again, then demanding Richard Branson's personal e-mail address (and not getting it) and then giving up.

But it *was* bonkers.

And I don't mean how much time and effort was spent on trying to rectify the problem that Virgin had created.

I mean that Virgin would NOT back down, even despite admitting guilt, and even when we suggested that they offered the luxury upgrade to another family instead.

Or better still... give it to us as well.

They just wouldn't budge!

Which I actually suspect our friends were really praying would be the case.

"No, Mr YTS kid, YOU listen to me... give that five thousand pound upgrade to a much nicer resort to someone else as we really don't want it (we do really) as we want to stay with our friends (not really, just give us the upgrade) and you're about to ruin the holiday we've all been looking forward to all year (not really, in fact you've actually just made it better as we're getting a much better resort than the shit hole we were going to be staying in and we're not paying any more for it) and not only that but you're going to have four VERY unhappy kids to have to deal with (they'll get over it) and they'll all be flying out on the same plane and I wouldn't wish that on anyone (but as we're in business class now you can just ply us with champagne for the whole flight and the kids get to watch TV for ten hours... so who gives a shit)!"

No wonder they didn't do anything!

So day one of our holiday and the Ipad was out and the wife was looking at holidays for next year.

DAY ONE!

And not with Virgin I'll hasten to add.

Although as Virgin *was* the cheapest yet again it turned out that it was with Virgin!

So much for showing them honey!

I never really got bored working at show grounds or exhibition halls as the shows or exhibitions only lasted a few days and then I was off to pastures greener.

Plus, there's *always* something exciting happening.

And plus, you're usually surrounded by glamorous looking people -- and of course I mean *women* and not the freaks that go to some of these things.

I worked at the *'Caravan and Camping Show'* once and was amazed at how many people wandered around with pictures of their motor homes knitted into their woollen jumpers.

I kid you not!

Like that was the fashion trend amongst those jet setters of modern day society.

And there's often the odd celebrity walking around the bigger shows.

And I mean *proper* celebrities and not one of those 'Big Brother' or 'Get Me Out of Here' freaks that none of us have really ever heard of or if we did vaguely recognise the name might remark 'oh, yeah, I remember him... thought he was dead!'

So this brings me on nicely to the time when I almost got imprisoned for treason.

As you do!

I was working at one of these shows and was very privileged to be positioned in the fenced off area next to the Royal Enclosure and as if luck would have it, Her Maj and Phil had also popped in to see the show.

Now I have *seen* the queen, in the flesh (not literally -- thankfully!) a few times before as one of our friends is COMPLETELY bonkers about her and literally follows her everywhere, but there's generally always been a crowd and some very large people carrying big guns in between us.

The first time I saw her (in the flesh) was when she was swapping from her nice comfy limo to her horse drawn carriage so she could arrive in style at the races.

Like as if she doesn't normally arrive in style wherever she goes eh?!

Apparently, as the carriage isn't all that comfortable (I guess sitting on solid gold seats probably is likely to give the most blue blooded of them piles after a little while -- perhaps they should just stuff the pillows with more money?!) she cheats a little and drives most of the way in comfort and then swaps for the last, *smaller* part of the journey so that everyone can see her arrive in a gold plated horse drawn carriage and then remember just how rich she actually is.

And if you know where it is she swaps over, you can go and watch.

And our friend did!

Because she knows all of the spots.

Because she's besotted by her.

So on one such occasion we got invited to join our friend and ALL the other crazies at this particular (secret) area of woodland early in the morning and so we turn up there and then simply set up camp for the day and wait for her to arrive.

There were easily over a hundred people there and everyone knew each other as they're all members of this secret, invite only, cult.

Plus all of their kids were there as well as none of them go to school because they're all home schooled which is the only way they can travel all over the country following the queen wherever she goes.

They can't have the inconvenience of school (or kids) getting in their way!

And also because kids can carry deckchairs.

You see they all love to do a little gambling.

By the edge of the road was a long row of deckchairs, camping seats, stools -- in fact anything that could double as a seat.

And not to sit on.

Oh no.

So they could bagsy a spot in the hope that when Her Maj did pull up, one of those lucky stalkers would have gambled right and put their green and white striped deckchair in exactly the right place so they could be as close as someone could get to the figure head of our great country for when she bounded out of her car for the switch over.

It was like being on holiday with a whole bunch of mad Germans that didn't so much claim the sun lounger with their beach towels but instead staked their claim to the actual ground... and *with* a sun lounger.

So my wife and I while away the hours before the big arrival listening to their stories of previous encounters and by encounters I actually mean brushes with her close protection officers, until about thirty minutes before and suddenly all these people start getting a bit restless like a horse that knows it's feeding time.

They start getting up.

Walking around.

Then pacing up and down.

All conversation stops.

It's like they're getting ready for a big fight.

And most of them are.

You see, it was coming up to twelve O'clock and she was apparently soon to arrive and they were now nervously hoping they'd gambled right.

And then her car pulls in to view and it's like that moment in the Tour de France when someone makes a well timed break and then everyone goes for it.

There's people rushing for their deckchairs -- throwing other chairs out of the way.

Fights are breaking out because someone's standing too close to someone else's sacred, and protected invisible space.

I mean five minutes ago all of these people were normal (I say 'normal') and respectable members of society swapping stories and sausage rolls and now they were quite prepared to kill each other.

All common decency had disappeared.

If I had somehow fallen asleep (there was no chance of that as they wouldn't stop talking to the newbie about who had had the best encounter) and woken up right at that exact moment I could have been forgiven for thinking that world war three had broken out, martial law had been imposed and the looting had already begun.

But oh no... this was all to see who could get the closest to Her Maj.

And all the time the car was slowly drawing nearer.

I did think it would be funny if the driver just drove slowly past and didn't stop, but I suspect he knew the chaos this would cause if he did and so decided it wasn't worth it.

I would have loved to have been a fly on the wall in the back of that car.

So the car slows down.

The close protection officers line up trying to bring this OAP riot to some kind of control.

And this just makes them go even crazier because it's obvious now that the very start of the viewing line has gambled poorly and clearly missed out so they all start pushing their way up the line trying desperately to keep up with the car as it creeps past them.

Well this causes everything to kick off.

People are shouting at each other.

The top part of the viewing line starts pushing back.

People are getting squashed.

People are falling over.

And we're just standing back, well out of the way, watching in amazement as it all unfolds before our very eyes.

Even our friend, who's normally an upstanding pillar of the local community, is rolling up her sleeves and getting stuck in.

People are shoving and pushing.

I half expect the close protection officers to pull Uzi's from under their jackets and just finish everyone off.

And I bet they wish they could as well!

And then the driver, who's probably realised he's caused enough bloodshed already, finally stops the car.

The horses and cart stop behind.

And they wait for the crowd to calm down.

It's like being back at school again.

'Fingers on lips everyone!'

Eventually normality is restored.

And then a door opens and out pop a few dignitaries -- who no one recognises.

And then Phil.

There's a huge cheer.

Flags start waving.

The calls of 'Hello Sir!' ring out from the crowd.

And then the other door opens and there's Her Maj in all her glory.

All four foot of it.

And the crowd go mad -- as dignifiedly as they can, but then just think 'SOD IT' and whoever can make the biggest fool of themselves will surely gain her attention.

"Hello Mam!" -- even louder than for Phil (I guess he's used to that).

"Over here Mam, it's me Jenny! Remember me... from the other time!!"

There's bunches of flowers and gifts being handed to close protection officers to give to her, which I'm sure they just bin -- or take home to their wives.

And so it goes on.

All these hanger-oners wanting recognition and all secretly hoping that Her Maj is going to like the look of one of them and invite them to join her on her day out.

Which of course is NEVER going to happen as she too thinks they're all raving loons!

So she does that awkward smile thing she does when she's surrounded by her peasants.

Attempts a feeble wave.

And then climbs in the carriage and whispers something to the driver -- which I just assume is *get me the hell out of here!*

And in the blink of an eye she's literally *outta there*.

Gone!

Leaving everyone to turn to each other and then, rather bizarrely, just carry on as civilly as before she arrived.

Like those last ten minutes didn't just happen.

Polite conversation.

Cucumber sandwiches.

A tipple of white wine.

Madness!

So, I'm on the stand next to the Royal Enclosure and one particular escaped loon has taken up far too much of my time so I'm now bursting for the loo.

And being staff, so to speak, my pass allows me to use the ones in the VIP marquee at the back of the stands.

No stinking portaloo for me with its faulty lock and lack of soap or toilet paper!

No siree!

So I venture innocently in.

And the toilets are certainly fit for a king.

Or rather a prince.

And I figure I may as well take advantage of this fact, so I take my time.

Use both the Molton Brown hand soap AND the moisturiser.

When in Rome!

The scent of vanilla and honey on my hands will show all those blue loo users that I've finally made something of my life!

No crapping over a bucket anymore for me.

And realising that I've probably been in there for forty five minutes now, if not longer, I figure I'd better head back to the stand, so I wander casually out into the corridor and stroll slowly over to the main entrance.

And I notice there's a bit of a crowd gathering.

And some commotion.

And I realise that Her Maj is on her way in.

And I'm going to have to pass her.

Maybe even *squeeze* my way past her.

Can I do that?!

I mean, is that acceptable?!

Am I allowed to *literally* brush shoulders with the queen?

And before I can answer my own question a close protection office steps out in front of me, jolly fellow he was, and asks me rather politely if I'd *'hang on a minute as the queen's on her way in'*.

No shit the queen's on her way in.

The only thing that was missing was a fanfare.

And Corgis.

So naturally I agree and so he and I and a few others caught up in the same predicament stand to the side so she and her cronies can head past us without the risk of having to get too close to one of us and possibly catch something.

And never having been in this predicament before I'm a little nervous.

I mean I've seen enough celebrities now to not be all that star struck but a member of the Royal Family and in particular the head honcho... well that's something else.

And as she passes she casts me a look.

Well, more of a glare.

And we make eye contact.

Share a moment!

And I don't really know what to do so I simply smile and remembering that when in the presence of royalty you're supposed to do something....

So I curtsey.

And she glares at me.

And then something hits me (and not the copper standing next to me either).

A thought.

And that thought suddenly takes on a life of its own.

Dangerously starts growing inside my head.

Now I don't know if you've ever been in a real important situation.

A situation that you wouldn't normally be in and therefore have no real time to prepare for it.

Or even get accustomed to it.

But one that you somehow *find* yourself in and there's a particular way you should act but nerves get the better of you or you just don't have a bloody clue, and then your mind gets involved and before you know it, it starts 'suggesting things'.

Which probably explains why people do the craziest of stuff that all gets caught on camera.

Well, I'm standing there.

The Queen is walking right in front of me.

Yes, there's someone with a gun standing next to me but he's not restraining me and his gun is holstered -- I hope!

And she's now just giving me the evils.

And with all that going on this thought flashes into my mind....

'I COULD BUNDLE HER RIGHT NOW!'

And no one would be able to stop me!

And then I begin having this internal conversation with myself.

'Don't be stupid!'

'No, go on do it!'

'No, don't be ridiculous!'

'Go on, it'll be hilarious!'

'No it won't!'

'Yes, it will -- you'll be a hero!'

'I'll be banged up!'

'So! Just think of the stories. Think of the fame!'

And then I'm conscious that I'm actually having this conversation with myself.

And not entirely out loud but I'm clearly giving off all the facial expressions as I clock Her Maj's somewhat puzzled look as she's continues staring at me as she passes.

And luckily for me, and all that is holy, a hand pats me on the shoulder.

"Thanks a lot mate!"

The close protection officer's voice brings me back to reality and before I have time to say *'hey, this'll make you laugh....'* he's off to make sure there's no more fruitcakes about to try and get a free piggy back off the queen.

So I wander back out to the stand and tell my little story to all my fellow workers but of course no one believes me.

And why would they?

It is an unbelievable story.

Particularly as we all know that under normal circumstances none of us peasants would be allowed such unrestricted access to this country's greatest figure head.

But little do they know that me and Her Maj did share a moment together -- but not for the right reasons.

And I bet all those fruit loops at that bit of woodland would be really jealous if only they knew.

I can't wait to tell them when we all hook up again next year!

I'll be there with my little white and green deckchair.

In fact I'll be taking four of them -- one for each member of the family.

Well the kids will be with us of course as there's more chance of me getting close to her if they help out a bit.

And this time I wonder if Her Maj will remember ME?!

Chapter Seventeen

A & E

The wife's entry

Never catch a falling tray!

Particularly if that tray is falling out of an open oven.

And particularly if that oven has been sitting at two hundred degrees for the past twenty minutes cooking a pie.

I figured that was advice my husband would appreciate as we sat in the accident and emergency waiting room together -- his hand plunged into a bucket full of iced water.

"So why weren't you wearing oven gloves again?"

Turns out he was only checking on the baking progress of the pie when he opened the oven door and so didn't actually need to remove anything from the hot oven.

It also turns out that next time he won't simply pile all the other baking trays on top of one another at the bottom of the oven so then when you yank the sticking oven door open the vacuum it creates causes the unbalanced and unevenly sized baking trays that are precariously rammed on top of one another to fall out.

No.

He'll stack them neatly like I keep telling him to instead.

Another favourite of his is to put things back into cupboards where they just don't go.

"Do you actually live in this house?"

"What?"

"Well, this doesn't go there!"

"Well I didn't know where it went and you wanted me to empty the dishwasher!"

In typical husband fashion he'll huff and puff his way through emptying the dishwasher almost as much as he does when I ask him to put the ironing (that I do) away, clearly hating the fact that I've asked him to do it to help me out as I struggle through the door with the shopping I've just spent hours gathering at the local supermarket before I then start cooking him his dinner, getting the kids ready to go back out the door to their many afterschool clubs while sorting out their school things for tomorrow and in between all the other motherly and housewifey things I have to do on top of holding down a job and helping him run his business.

Otherwise it won't get done.

"Can't we just get a second dishwasher?"

That way, apparently, we could simply use the clean plates from one dishwasher and then put them in the second dishwasher when they get dirty again.

Genius!

And such a simple answer to such a simple problem as well.

Great work Einstein!

What's next… the wheel?

Until of course I remind him that not only is that a ridiculous suggestion but where would we put a second dishwasher anyway?

Outside?!

In order for us to fit a second dishwasher amongst the already cluttered kitchen cupboards, we'd have to have a new kitchen built which, and I naturally assume now, wouldn't be cheap.

And why stop at dishwashers?

Let's get two washing machines while we're at it.

One for whites and one for colours.

That way we don't have to waste time putting them into a laundry bin and then, God forbid, having to separate them out ready for washing.

We could just put them straight into the correct, colour coded washing machine and Bob's your uncle.

And you know what, by the momentary look in his eye I think he would have actually gone for it where it not for one small thing....

He doesn't actually know how to use the washing machine!

I received a frantic call one day in the office.

"It's your husband on the line, there's some kind of an emergency!"

So, naturally as it was an emergency, I apologised to my colleagues, put the weekly marketing meeting on hold and took his frantic phone call on the meeting room phone -- in front of my sales team.

"What's happened, are the kids okay?!"

"Yes."

"Is it my parents?!"

"No."

"Are *you* okay?!"

"No!"

My heart missed a beat as I feared the worst.

Something was wrong with my husband.

Heart attack!

He's having a heart attack!

And he's on his own in the house.

Oh my God!

"What! What is it?!" I frantically asked, as I'm already cramming everything back into my bag, slipping my jacket back on one arm and rushing out the door, still attached to the phone.

And all while my colleagues are hanging on to my every word!

"I can't get this bloody washing machine to work!"

"What?!"

"I know, and I need to get my trainers clean for tomorrow!"

Well he did have a bloody heart attack when I got back home that night so needless to say I've now had his calls barred when I'm at work.

What is it with husbands and white goods anyway?

If it had 'PlayStation' on the front he'd have known how to use it without even having to read the instructions.

I thought we'd won the lottery the other day.

"Oh my God, honey, quick, come and look!"

Now, I've learnt, over the many years, that when my husband verbally expresses his excitement to the point where he's literally having an orgasm, if he's doing it in front of the PC and if the PC is in full view of the kids at the time, not to rush over all that quickly.

And once again I was right.

"It's a washing machine?!" I commented -- a little too unenthusiastically for his liking it would appear.

"Not just any old washing machine my sweet... this one can wash duvets!"

Now, for as long as I can remember.

Over the forty odd years that I've been alive on this planet.

I can't ever recall....

EVER!

Having to wash a duvet.

Not once!

In fact, if ever there was one, now completely forgotten about, one off occasion when, as a much younger and consequently weaker bladdered individual, one of our children, having had a little too much milk before bedtime, could possibly have had a little accident in the night... I'd have sent the duvet off to the dry cleaners for a fiver.

In fact it would actually be cheaper to keep the existing washing machine and just buy a new duvet if ever one of ours needed washing.

In fact we could buy four new duvets every year.

One for us.

One for each of the kids.

And one for the bloody cats for the amount we'd save on NOT buying this ridiculously oversized, no where to put it, washing machine.

Especially as we'd need to get the utility room extended if I were to have a momentary lapse of sensibility and somehow allow my husband to buy it.

And it would only be me using it as he wouldn't have a bloody clue anyway.

And so this is pretty much how my life goes.

My husband, being the gadget loving freak that he is, thinks that in some sort of weird, making up for his overspending on useless gadgets that we don't need, kind of way, if he buys me something, a gadget of my very own as well every now and again, he'll not only keep me sweet but the karmic balance will once again be restored as I'll be so blinded by his act of kindness that I'll turn a blind eye to anything else he then buys (wastes) for himself.

He clearly doesn't know me at all!

And he is forever buying the latest, useless gadgets or the newest technology, which is generally when it's still all in its earliest and therefore most likely to pack up and go wrong stage.

Last Christmas he bought me some battery powered, heated gloves for the winter months.

Now I say they were for me only I didn't actually get to wear them.

Not once.

Because they were so novel that he just had to try them out first.

And then so did both the kids.

Plus, he didn't actually go for the expensive pair, like they use when they have to ride motorbikes in the dead of winter and it's either pay through the nose for heated gloves or lose your fingers to frostbite.

No!

In typical husband fashion he bought the cheapest pair he could find which were so bad that no sooner had you switched on the heat function, set the house alarm and locked the front door, the battery had gone flat and they needed re-charging.

I think they may have once made it to the top of the driveway.

I caught him looking for a drone once.

Yes, that's right... a drone!

Our son is ten now and consequently in the final year of his school and so is therefore undergoing much peer pressure to start walking to school on his own.

At least that's what *he* tells us anyway.

Much like he was under much peer pressure to have his own e-mail address.

"So let me get this right... you're at school all day with these kids, in fact thinking about it you spend more hours each week with them than you do with your own family and yet, when you get home you then need to commence e-mailing each other as well?"

Apparently so.

And not only that but he's the only child at school that doesn't have his own e-mail address and so not only is he missing out on such breaded cat related imagery, he's also getting ridiculed about being the only one in school without his own e-mail address and that's causing him stress which could affect his otherwise good grades.

Apparently!

Well after months of this emotional bribery my husband eventually succumbed and tried to set up an e-mail address for him only to discover that at ten years old the *'authorities'* consider him too young to have (and in my opinion, even need) his own e-mail address.

But apparently all his mates have got e-mail addresses and their (much kinder) parents have set them up in their name but with an e-mail address relating to their child so it looks like it's their own one.

So we did.

And thus his e-mail account was born.

And guess what.

He's the only one in the whole school with e-mail.

In fact it was so bad that I had to e-mail him otherwise he'd have never received a thing.

He'd bounce downstairs each morning telling my husband to get off the PC as he needed to check his e-mail before school.

And I was still the ONLY person e-mailing him!

He does get e-mail now.

In fact he gets quite a bit.

In his defence he's actually worked quite hard on getting his e-mail address out there into cyberspace.

And he's done it by registering with all those crappy competitions from his comics and being sure to tick the box that says he DOES want them to contact him.

He's the only person I know of in the whole world that is not just happy, but actually ecstatic when he gets SPAMMED!

So I click on Amazon one day and get hit with floods of adverts for drones.

"Have you been looking at Drones, on Amazon?" I innocently enquire in the general direction of my husband.

"Oh... yeah," he nonchalantly replies, as if this question was typical of the weird everyday questions that get asked in our household.

"And *why* may I ask?"

"Well, because the military ones were too expensive!"

So when I eventually explain what I meant it turns out that he did have a very good reason for wanting to buy a drone....

So he could follow overhead as our son walked to school on his own.

Well it's only a mile and a half to school from where we live apparently.

My husband genuinely thought that he could wave goodbye to our son on the doorstep, sprint into the kitchen and launch the drone from his laptop and the comfort of the breakfast table.

And to think that I would have actually had a concern had my husband informed me that he was planning to follow a few hundred yards behind our son, hiding behind parked cars and hedgerows so as not to be spotted when our son was eventually allowed to walk to school with his mates.

Because that wouldn't have looked suspicious at all.

No!

Instead, he thinks it's far better to have some military style drone follow overhead projecting live images of our son and his mates back to the kitchen as they innocently head off to school on their own.

All in the name of keeping an eye on them.

And the only reason he didn't buy one?

Because there are currently no, bought it off the internet, camera mounted spy drones, available that travel further than the end of your garden.

Honestly, what useless MI5, 007 style secret agent is ever going to buy a spy drone to use to spy on people when the only person he'll ever actually be able to use it to spy on with... is himself?!

And my son's just as bad as he thought it was a great idea.

But then again he also thought he could ride it to school.

Disappointed to learn that he couldn't he did come back with the next best thing to overcome the drones underachieving distance related issues.

"Don't worry mum, I'll carry it to school for dad and then when I get there let it go."

"What?! That's just as bad!"

"Is it?"

"Of course it is, because they only work as far as the end of the driveway so that means your dopey father will then have to go and collect it, so he might as well have just walked you to school!"

My husband and I visited the ideal home exhibition not long after we bought our first house together as we thought it would be a good place to go and look for a sofa.

We didn't have a sofa.

We needed one.

We'd had no real luck finding one we both liked during all of our weekend sofa shopping outings and three, maybe even four weeks into it, and we're talking way before the days of the internet don't forget, we were getting really frustrated.

And I have to say as much as we loved each other dearly, we could have just as easily gotten divorced over this bloody sofa hunting.

I liked one which of course he hated.

He loved one which of course I hated.

Mainly because the only ones he liked plugged in to the electrics, massaged you using several varying types of massage, had built in speakers in the headrests and a fridge , just large enough for a six-pack of lager, built in to the arm rests.

Oh, and there was only enough room on it for one.

And it cost the price of a small family saloon.

So casually flicking through the Sunday paper one weekend I noticed an advert for the London Ideal Home exhibition.

We'd both actually worked there many years ago in our former careers and so we instantly knew it would be the ideal (excuse the pun) place to go and find our perfect sofa.

Why hadn't we thought of this before?!

It was the perfect answer to our otherwise imperfect sofa searching troubles.

So we took the cash we'd been given by all of friends and family for the housewarming party we had thrown a month or so earlier.

Battled out way through London traffic.

To eventually arrive at The Earls Court Exhibition Centre (is London Traffic ever quiet?! -- there are traffic jams at three O'clock in the morning for God's sake).

Parked up in the exhibition hall's underground car parking (rip off) facilities.

And strolled casually, hand in hand, into the exhibition hall and in search of a brand new sofa and the final piece of our lifelong, everlasting happiness together.

And we walked out with a plasma TV instead.

Or rather he did.

Along with a surround system and amplifier.

So we had this forty six inch, completely unnecessary flat screen TV and nothing to actually sit and watch it on.

Yes, he's a salesman's dream.

But it doesn't end there.

Oh no!

He then had it wall mounted.

In his defence, and to save on costs, he did it himself, with the help of several of his mid-lifers and... not because he needed help drilling in the brackets or assistance on using an angle grinder to remove chunks of perfectly good plaster from the wall.

No.

Because it was so bloody heavy, it took three of them to lift it.

And of course, after all the mess he'd made cutting out the groves in which to hide all of the wires and whatever else needed hiding away, we had to have the lounge re-decorated.

And before you ask, no, he couldn't actually redecorate the lounge himself as, to be honest, you've probably gathered by now based on his DIY skills (or rather... limits) that if he'd have redecorated it, it would have looked far worse than how it looked right now and we'd have still had to have gotten someone else in who actually knows what they're doing, to re-do it.

We had a relatively new car once and as it was new, it came with a warranty.

After about twelve months of owning it, it had to be serviced and one thing the dealership said we needed to have done was the brake fluid changing and they could do this at the same time as the service for an extra 'one hundred pounds'.

"ONE HUNDRED POUNDS!!! -- I'll do it myself!"

I cringe now when I hear those words float effortlessly out of his mouth.

"Just pay it and get it done properly!"

"NEVER!"

So, he and another of his mid-lifers, who apparently knows something about cars, which I personally think is simply how to drive them as everything he's ever fixed on all our other cars have then had to be re-fixed by someone who actually knows what they are doing, attempted, with the help of the internet, to change the brake fluid.

And in an attempt to prove to me that they had done a good job....

And because I refused to ever drive it again....

Took it for a spin round the block and arrived back ten minutes later, amazingly, still in one piece.

So we drove the car to its service and pleased as punch my husband announced.

"Don't worry about the brake fluid... I've had it done. And for half the price *you* quoted!"

He kicks back in the swivel chair.

Now I do love him.

And I particularly love his little quirks.

"Can't wait to tell that rip off service department where to go with its stupid, unnecessary brake fluid change!" he kept announcing, all the way up.

A huge satisfied grin slapped all over his smug face.

"Oh, okay," replied the actually sweet and trustworthy looking service department man.

"And did they use approved brake fluid?"

Now I love it when my husband's stuck for words.

That moment when I cast a glance his way and watch, with amusement, as his eyes widen slightly and I can sense his brain going into overdrive as it desperately searches all its archives for a reply that will end his immediate suffering.

You know when you were at school and the naughty kids were messing about on the back row and the teacher had just asked the class a question and they clearly weren't listening and the teacher has spotted this so calls one of them out in front of the whole class and ask them what the answer is, or better still, what the question was.

Well it was that moment all over again.

I see him swallow nervously.

"Errr… it was in a black bottle."

I lean back in my chair now to watch the show.

"Dot four or dot five?"

"I'm not sure!"

"Did the garage stamp the service book to validate the warranty?"

A bead of sweat runs down his forehead.

"Well I actually did it myself."

"Oh… and are you an approved, VAT registered mechanic?"

So we had the brake fluid changed for a second time that week and it was more expensive than originally quoted because he and his dopey mate had actually damaged one of the nuts, or something, so that had to be repaired as well.

Plus, with what he spent originally, giving his mate a tenner for his help, it actually cost us *double* the originally quoted price.

So the plasma TV took pride of place, mounted on the wall and we consequently had to re-position all of our furniture as it became apparent that modern day rectangular lounges aren't really designed to accommodate a wall mounted TV as the TV sits down one side of the room, the sofa (when we eventually got one) sits opposite the TV thus leaving a huge void at the other end as all of the living now takes place at the TV end.

I also have to laugh at my husband as the only time he's truly happy having people round is when we've either just had something, some refurb or modernisation done to the house, or when he's just bought some latest gadget and wants to show it off.

So friends arrived and for a change we had pre-dinner drinks in the lounge before moving into the dining room to tuck into his signature dishes -- again!

It was of course standing room only as we had nowhere for everyone to sit yet which, bless them, no one commented on which was a surprise as we did have somewhere to sit in the kitchen, which is where we normally have our pre-dinner drinks -- unless of course we've had another room modernised, as was the case.

I have to admit, pre-dinner drinks in our bedroom was the strangest.

"I love your TV!" one of the guests fatally commented.

Well that was it.

It was like my husband had suddenly turned into a game show host or one of those presenters on those ridiculous late night roulette gambling shows where it's clear they have to adlib for thirty minutes but they really don't have anything to talk about so it all just comes out as waffle.

Painful!

So I listened for the thousandth time as to how much it had cost and his incredibly detailed description about how he had hidden all the wires into the wall so it looked just like a picture frame hanging there.

Yeah, a bloody expensive picture frame.

In fact I'd have actually rather had a Rembrant hanging there and instead kept our perfectly, nothing wrong with it at all and relatively normal sized, normal TV instead.

"So is it High Definition ready as I read somewhere that you shouldn't buy a plasma TV unless it's High Definition ready?"

"What?!"

And so we revert back to the service department moment again.

And guess what?

It wasn't High Definition ready.

Of course it wasn't.

There was another stand at the ideal home exhibition that *was* selling High Definition TV's though.

And we did visit that stand.

And listen to the sales guy tell us ALL about them.

And even he said *'whatever you do, don't buy a plasma TV unless it's High Definition ready.'*

But as they were more expensive, and my husband's all about saving money, as you know, plus, he thought it was just a sales pitch, we went for the cheaper one instead.

But all is not lost apparently because when High Definition is eventually launched then all we'll need to do is buy a new High Definition TV, remove our old (useless) none High Definition TV from the wall, feed the new cables through the channelling in the wall and simply swap them over.

Job done!

That is, it would have been job done....

Had it not have been for the small, minute, tiny little fact that my dopey husband and his dopey mid-lifer friends didn't actually create any channelling in the wall for additional cables to be fed through at some later, TV replacing stage of our lives.

No.

They simply carved away half the bloody lounge wall.

Shoved all the cables in the grove.

And then plastered them all back in again.

And so of course not being one to have his friends ridicule him for owning such out of date technology, I find myself, less than twelve months later, answering the door to the local high street TV specialists and EXPERTS, who have brought our new, High Def and future proofed TV round to professionally install it for us.

And I say us....

I actually mean ME!

Because there's no way I can go through all that again as I've just heard that 3D TV is on now its way!

Chapter Eighteen

We're Going On A Bear Hunt

The husband's entry

I took up flying a while back.

My wife, and a few of my other, so called 'friends' (now demoted to acquaintances) were a little unkind about it and referred to it in the same vein as they do most other *'out the out of character'* things I do....

'Mid-life crisis!'

But here's the thing about the old mid-life crisis.

It's not an attempt at regaining lost youth.

Or even a sad attempt at doing, or buying something that you feel you've missed out on.

The truth about the mid-life crisis is simply the fact that the vast majority of us could never afford to buy a Porsche, or a motorbike or learn to fly or whatever else it is that we get branded 'mid life crisis' for in our early twenties and so it takes us until we're in the middle stage of our life before we can.

If I were to have highlights in my hair.

Get my ear pierced.

Even get a tattoo.

Or maybe even swap my wife for a girl half my age (like I dare!).

Then THAT could be classed as a mid life crisis because those are the kind of things you would be able to do when you were in your twenties.

But learning to fly can actually be done at any age.

The only criteria is... you have to be able to afford to do it.

And of course have the spare time.

So the kids are at school all day now and I'm often *'working from home'* a bit more and also have a bit of surplus cash, so naturally the circumstances were all right.

And so I started learning to fly at a local flying school.

Anyway, on one particular occasion I arrived for my lesson and before I continue I perhaps should tell you that the chief instructor at this school was an idiot.

He looked like a dirtier and older version of Spike Milligan – just before he died.

And he was probably twice his age!

Dandruff all over his shoulders.

That dank smell of unwashed clothes.

And did I mention that he was an idiot?

A female friend of mine learnt to fly there a few years before me, in fact it was her that recommended the school to me, and she was blonde and slim and funnily enough he took her on as one of his students.

In fact he only taught the females as he thought himself a bit of a ladies' man.

Anyway, he was an idiot and so I arrived at the school and reception was, as it always was, rather busy.

Pilots and students were coming and going, and as I was signing in I clocked this guy leaning against the counter opposite.

Bit of a dude.

Styled hair.

Popped collars.

Aviators on his head.

A bit like Tom Cruise when he was in Top Gun.

You get the picture.

As there were always people milling around that I didn't know I just assumed he was a pilot so gave him the customary nod and looked around for my instructor.

At which point old Spike Milligan bounded over.

"Ha ha, here he is (punching me on the arm and gesturing to Tom)... hey you two should have a fight!"

Tom just very coolly lifts his eyes in our direction.

"Yeah, I'd put my money on you (Tom) though!"

So I'm thinking all the usual things I tend to think about Spike including, *'it really is time they carted you off to the OAP home'*, and then my instructor appears and Spike drags him into his hilarious comedy show he's now performing.

"What do you think? These two should have a fight, shouldn't they?!" -- as he nudges him with his elbow.

My instructor's awkward smile now matches mine and even old wrinkle free, cool as a cucumber Tom looks like he's had enough as *'not quite so hilarious as the original Spike'* Spike, continues his barrage of jokes at my expense.

And by now he has a bit of an audience and because he's the boss, those that rely on him to pay their wages act like they think he's hilarious -- as is often the case.

And Spike's in for the long haul now but thankfully no longer at my expense as my instructor gives me a quick out by suggesting we get started otherwise he'll run over for his next student and consequently drags me away and so Spike starts showing off in front of Tom at someone else's expense instead.

So inside the Spike free comfort zone of our little briefing room we get started.

A few minutes into it and I clock Tom heading off outside with Spike and I just have to ask....

"Who was that guy... a pilot?"

My instructor leans back in his chair.

"Do you not know who that was?"

Well unless Tom Cruise has somehow managed to find the fountain of youth!

"No."

"Bear Grylls -- that was Bear Grylls, he's flying off to do some filming somewhere."

Now I had heard of Bear Grylls, as most of us have as he's never off the bloody tele (or the book shelves), but I'd just never seen a photo of him, let alone watched any of his TV shows so naturally I wouldn't have had a clue what he looked like.

And clearly didn't.

And even if I did, so what?!

Y'see I'm one of those guys that will never approach someone famous.

My wife would, in fact I have to keep hold of her whenever we do see someone famous as she'll happily bound over and make a fool of herself (and me) if I don't.

I took her for dinner once at Claridges and Kyle and Dannii (Minogue) were sat with a load of people on the next table and all night my wife wanted to go over and say 'hi' but I said I'd disown her if she did.

And of course 'it would only be her... they wouldn't mind! After all they seem quite nice on the tele!'

Of course they do!

What kind of celebrity, that wants everyone to like them, is going to come across as a right arsehole on TV?

Isn't that right Katie Price?

And I guarantee that EVERYONE in the restaurant also thought the same thing.

No one wants to be disturbed in that way do they?!

Can you imagine being out with friends or worse, your family, and have person after person approaching you and asking for an autograph or a photo -- or both.

Maybe even sitting down to join you.

At one point, some fruit loop and incredibly inconsiderate diner did approach and had a brief chat with them and a few minutes later they, along with the rest of the table, got up and left.

Well done!

And I can't blame them.

Us, non-famous people think it would be great to have all that fame.

Be recognised wherever you go.

But I'm telling you that it would soon wear off.

And fast.

Plus, they always say you should never meet your hero's.

Michael Mcintyre sat down next to me on the steps in front of the lighthouse as me and the family watched the Jonny Thunder show at Legoland in Windsor a few years ago.

And I *loved* him.

Thought he was one of the funniest guys on TV.

And I was desperate to speak to him.

To tell him that I thought he was brilliant.

But fear of rejection got the better of me and so instead, and in a real lame attempt to instigate a conversation, I turned to him and said *'s'cuse me mate, any chance you could move your pizza box so my kid can sit there?!'*

BRILLIANT!

Well done me.

A great ice breaker and what a well thought up opening line to spark up a conversation with one of the UK's greatest comics.

Anyway he reluctantly moved it amidst a lot of (very well spoken) huffing and puffing and shaking of his head.

He'd probably put it there so I *couldn't* get too close to him.

But then of course it's all ruined isn't it?!

That image we have of our hero's.

In an instant!

Because Mike didn't say, *'of course, how terribly inconsiderate of me... let me make it up to you with these free tickets to my next sell out tour --*

now would you like to come back to the hotel with me and order canapé's!' I now think he's an arse!

Although God knows what *he* thinks of *me*.

But at least he knows I exist!

We shared a moment together and we'll always have that!

My wife took me to see Derren Brown a few years back (I do love him as well) and we made a bit of a night of it by staying in a hotel.

Well it turns out that he was staying in the same hotel as us as well (thank you receptionist) and so we went for breakfast the next day and there he was.

And they stuck us on the table *next* to him.

And I desperately wanted to tell him that I loved his show last night.

But didn't.

Perhaps I should have, I don't know... but I didn't.

And I'm sure he's probably grateful for that.

Although if he was any good he probably already knew the dilemma I was having and should have just dropped a signed photo of himself on my table as he left.

So I missed my chance with Bear and it was probably a good thing to be honest because what would I have spoken to him about really?

What original question *hasn't* he been asked?

In my head we would have had the most enlightening of conversation all mixed in with light witty banter... but the reality is he would have thought me another one of those loons he desperately tries to avoid.

I do remember reading Derren Brown's book once and he actually devoted a section of it to the admiring letters he'd received over the years from so called 'fans'.

Weirdo's more like.

Scary!

And it backed up my belief that you shouldn't approach a celebrity.

It would almost have been better if I had started a conversation with Bear while not knowing who he was.

But then again, would that have been worse?

Would he have been thinking that I'm trying to play it *too* cool by talking to him like we're mates and not mentioning his fame?!

I did it once.

I was working at a show and one of the model / dancers came onto the stand but she was dressed in Salvation Army gear as part of her act (which I didn't know) and I innocently asked her *'how long had she worked for the salvation army*?' and well... let's just say it didn't go down too well!

But how was I to know?

Don't wear the bloody uniform out and about then!

So I got home and Googled Bear and he has quite the impressive bucket list and one thing, as we all know....

He's an expert on wilderness survival skills.

AND.

He also runs wilderness survival weekend experiences.

So I looked to book myself on to one.

And then saw the price.

But by then I was quite in the mood for a survival weekend.

'Just imagine the discipline involved' I told my friends, while desperately trying to convince them to join me on it -- and mainly because it was cheaper with ten of us.

So after a great deal of hard work and utilising all of my persuasion skills and promising that they could pay me back in instalments, I managed to get nine of them to say yes!

So I booked one.

At half the price.

And by half the price I mean it was literally the cheapest one I could find on the net.

And there was a reason it was cheap.

Because it was crap!

So ten of us rolled up at our agreed meeting point -- a pub, a little earlier than planned... and we all agreed that as were here it would be rude not to!'

So we did.

We walked in to this deserted country pub that looked like that pub from *'An American Werewolf in London'* and as we entered the land lady greeted us all with a lovely smile and a really warm welcome....

"Oh GOD! Are you lot here for that stupid bloody survival weekend? I hope you haven't parked in my bloody car park. I told them I'm not having it. That's for punters that is and not you bloody lot. Park on the road. And not in front of my pub either. I don't want you lot...."

And on and on and on she went.

When she eventually stopped ranting I suggested she signed herself up as a Jehovah's Witness as she can clearly talk and breathe at the same time and would it be too much to ask for some drinks?

Well the thought of us spending money to help pay for the upkeep of this dilapidated old building we were in obviously gained us a few brownie points and she calmed down a little.

And so beer in hand, we waited for our host to arrive.

And we waited.

And we waited.

And we drunk.

And we drunk.

And then I started wondering if I'd got the dates wrong.

Or maybe even the meeting point.

And by this time we'd sunk quite a few beers as well and I had forgotten to mention to my lot that they had a strict 'NO DRINKING' rule on this survival weekend.

Oh well!

So eventually our host arrived and when I say *arrived* I mean he literally burst through the door, out of breath and red faced, like he *had* been running from a supernatural half man half wolf type creature.

"Sorry I'm late, I got lost!"

Which I didn't think was the greatest opening line from someone that was going to show us how to survive in the middle of nowhere.

So he had just enough time to tell us that we shouldn't be drinking and then went off to appease the pissed off landlady.

Good luck with that I though and ordered another beer.

He returned ten minutes later apologised again for his tardiness, told us to stop drinking and then informed us that he was really pissed off because he was supposed to be running this with two more of his colleagues but they've let him down and so now it's just us and him.

But not to worry because he was an expert in wilderness survival and by the end of this so will we be.

We didn't really care!

So if we just put the beers down like he'd already told us and then all venture outside we can head off.

So we told *him* to venture outside while *we* finish our pints.

And he did.

A few minutes later and about six pints heavier we finally 'venture' outside all tingling with the thrill of adventure (or was it alcohol?), to join him.

And he's standing there, backpack at the ready, walking boots on, waiting.

"Gather round!"

We do.

And so he proceeds to go through the health and safety rules and regs, inform us that he'll be issuing us all with razor sharp hunting knives (which even I thought wouldn't be a wise move) and so that's why it's imperative we don't consume alcohol.

Too late I think mate!

And then he tells us to grab our stuff from our cars (which we've already decided are staying where they're parked!) and follow him.

Which we do.

Right to the other side of the car park.

"Right... this'll do!"

He drops his backpack next to a *very* small unlit camp fire.

We all look at each other expecting him to say... *'just kidding... ha ha, got you didn't I? We're really trekking over to the middle of those woods you can just about make out in the distance!'*

But oh no... we were going to be doing our survival weekend -- in a pub car park!

And all while people and cars were pulling in to the car park, narrowly avoiding running us over and all wondering what the bloody hell we were doing.

Which is exactly what *we* were wondering.

So our first task was to make some shelter for ourselves and no we weren't allowed to just book into the pub for the weekend because they wouldn't have a pub on a desert island now would they?!

They wouldn't have a pub car park either mate!

So he handed out some tarpaulin sheets and rope and told us to *'be creative'*.

So I tied mine up to the wing mirrors of two cars -- job done!

I did wonder whether I'd be so lucky as to find two cars in the wilderness if ever I was stranded but then again the chances of finding a tarpaulin and a rope would be just as unlikely.

Then we had to find something comfy to lie on and he suggested some of the ferns that were growing naturally along the sides of the road as they make a good mattress when they're all piled on top of one another.

And I had to agree that that would have been a great idea had it not been for the fact that I'd brought an airbed with me so I inflated that and the bonus was I could use the cigarette lighter attachment in the car to make it even easier.

The rest of my posse followed suit all while wannabe Bear Grylls watched on -- gob smacked.

And by the time we'd all neatly laid out our sleeping bags (some brought duvets with them) it was time for supper.

Wannabe Grylls handed out these very sharp hunting knives, read us all the health and safety points once again with a stern reminder of *'no alcohol!'* and then headed for the boot of his car.

We waited eagerly for him to return with the rabbit snares that we would be using to catch tonight's lunch and sure enough he returned a few minutes later....

With the rabbits!

Blimey... he's good I thought!

"Yeah, we're not allowed to snare rabbits in this country anymore so I bought some from my local butchers before I left."

WHAT?!

And apparently all we had to do was cut them up into small bits and throw them in the pot.

"I'll just go get some water from the pub while you do that!" he informed us.

Really?!

So you're planning on there being a pub on this desert island then... or perhaps just a fresh, clean running water supply?

And you're not actually going to show us how to cut these rabbits up then either?

So an hour or so later and we were all sitting on beer crates around a very small camp fire desperately trying to chew our way through the toughest boiled rabbit I've ever had while old Bear Grylls the second here proceeds to moan about how he's been dropped in the shit by his two colleagues and he was supposed to be teaching snowboarding this weekend but they conned him into this and moan, moan, moan.

We'll it's nice to know you're excited to be here!

So he finishes his rabbit, looks at his watch and then announces it's eleven o'clock and he's off and he'll see us in the morning.

And that's it.

"You're not staying the night with us?

"No, I've got a party to go to!"

And at that he gets in his car and pisses off.

And to make it worse the pub's now closed and we didn't bring alcohol as I was so paranoid that if we did and they caught us we'd be thrown off the course!

ARE YOU KIDDING ME!!!

And as we're in the middle of nowhere.

And we're all over the drink diving limit.

We can't drive anywhere to get any.

And we can't call a taxi as there's no mobile phone coverage.

Plus, even if we could, we're all dressed for a weekend in the woods and not for a classy wine bar in the nearest town.

And then it starts raining.

So all ten of us cram into the back of our cars and do our best to while away the hours until the morning which does eventually arrive.

So in an attempt to experience a real wilderness survival weekend half of us scour the roadside for wood to burn and the other half get the camp fire going again.

And before long we've got a real good blaze going.

And he'd also left us with his Gran's old stove kettle and as we were sensible enough to bring coffee with us, we're sorted until the pub opens at least.

And if I'm being honest I really didn't expect to see him again as they'd had our money but in all fairness his knackered old red Micra pulls back into the pub car park a few hours later.

And he jumps out.

And runs straight over to the camp fire.

And starts kicking it out.

"You can't have it that big... that was the agreement with the pub. Oh my God, she'll go mad if she sees it!"

And we all just watch -- gobsmacked ourselves now, as our lovely warm camp first is extinguished right before our very eyes!

So once he's calmed down he gets us all in a circle and starts to show us his whittling skills and how he can carve a spoon out of an old branch (that he's brought with him as we're not allowed to hack off any branches of the pub's trees either!).

And he proceeds to tell us how much of a skill this is and how you have to have excellent knife skills and having excellent knife skills is what will save your life if ever you do find yourself stranded in the wilderness.

And then as he's telling us all this... he slices his thumb.

Badly!

In fact -- VERY Badly!

But because he's been telling us all for the past thirty minutes about his *great knife skills* and because now would be a really weird stage for him to try to convince us that his spoon, that couldn't actually look any less like a spoon, and in fact looks more like my eight year old daughter has simply been hacking away at it, is finished, he pretends it didn't happen and just carries on whittling.

And obviously in loads of pain.

And at the same time trying to discreetly stop the spread of claret as it drips everywhere and hoping we don't notice.

Which of course we all do.

In fact, that's all we're staring at now.

Even his peeled stick is turning red.

And then no longer able to contain himself and because he's worried that Bear Grylls the second here may just be about to pass out from blood loss and one of us may have to give him mouth to mouth, one of my mates pipes up and says....

"Err... have you cut your thumb?"

And to which he replies....

"Yeah... I probably better get that seen to."

And so he dumps his wooden spoon, jumps in his car and heads off to A&E.

That's made the fire later I thought to myself!

So we're alone again and probably for the next few hours as well and the pubs now open so we do the only thing ten lost wilderness adventurers would do in our situation… we head inside.

And we're getting on alright with the landlady now and it turns out that despite being approached almost a year ago, this is the first wilderness survival weekend they've ever had here.

No kidding?

And by how it's all going so far it's clearly the first one *he's* ever done as well!

So we manage to do a deal on several bottles of good old Jack D and a load of beer and head back out to the campsite to hide them, just in case he returns with his 'no alcohol *my arse* rules!'

And eventually he does turn back up again.

And all stitched up as well.

And he's carrying a load of fish that's he's just picked up from Sainsbury's!

Yeah, because God forbid he'd have shown us how to actually catch a fish.

Plus, fishing's probably illegal here as well.

So at least he's going to show us how to prepare fish using the same knife that he almost cut his thumb off with and it's our last night and we're all tired and drunk and any ounce of respect or credibility this muppet once had has long since dried up, so we really couldn't give a shit anymore and just start taking the piss.

And he doesn't really know what to do.

But apparently he's going to stay tonight and unbeknown to us, there was a bit of a sheltered set up that he had already erected in the field behind the pub prior to us all arriving (and which we couldn't see), so he'll be staying there tonight -- well away from us!

So using a makeshift construction of entwined twigs to act like a grilling basket we desperately try to cook our badly filleted fish over the poxy small camp fire he's so precious about and of course my fish falls onto the floor -- right onto all the gravel and dirt.

But I'm so damn hungry I just pick it up and eat it anyway -- dirt and all.

And by now, even I've had enough.

And it's getting dark.

And I can't bear to listen to anymore of his bullshit stories about surviving in the wilderness and so we tell him *we're* all going to bed.

And it works a treat as he heads off to his camp.

So out comes the beer.

And the Jack Daniels.

And over to the camp fire comes anything that looks like it might burn.

And anything that doesn't for that matter.

And as everyone makes it there personal mission to get as shit faced as they can....

I make it my personal mission to get this fire going.

And I'm throwing everything on it now.

Beer crates.

Tyres.

Tarpaulin.

And it's going great guns.

In fact it's so bloody big now I'm sure they can see it from space.

In fact it actually becomes too hot to sit around so to prevent us all from getting third degree burns we're backed right away from it as we polish off yet another bottle of JD.

And then the unimaginable happens.

Old Bear Grylls comes running back over screaming *'what the hell are you doing! Put it out! Put it out!'*

But it's way too hot for him to get anywhere near so there's nothing he could do but stand there helpless and just watch.

Plus, we're much too drunk now to care, let alone help him.

And then he spots his Gran's stove kettle right in the middle of the flames and goes off on another one.

"Oh my God... my Gran's kettle. You've ruined it! You've RUINED IT!!"

It was true.

The whole thing was melting away quite nicely.

And then he clocks all the empty bottles of JD strewn around the campsite and just loses his bloody mind... "Oh my God! Oh MY GOD!! I told you lot no drinking! This is against the rules!"

And he starts tugging at his hair and jumping up and down.

"I'll get the sack!"

And then as he casts his sweaty little panicked gaze across the ten *'couldn't care less'* faces that stared back at him he realised he was fighting a losing battle and so with one last... *"y'know what... I'm done! You lot are on your own now!"* he retreats back to the safety of his own shelter.

ON OUR OWN!

Like this survival weekend was anything like it would have been had we actually been victims of a real life, landing on a desert island style, plane crash.

Like we had anything on 'LOST!'

Or CASTAWAY!

Where was 'Wilson' now?!

On our own are we mate?

Let me tell you something....

We've been on our own since you first arrived!

So we let him have thirty minutes to calm himself down and then we all sneak over to his tent.

And there he was... battery powered camp light illuminating his bedtime reading.

And remarkably his book of choice....

'The outdoor survival handbook' by Ray Mears.

In fact on closer inspection he was *surrounded* by wilderness survival books.

Ray Mears.

Bear Grylls (of course).

And a whole load of other authors that I'd never even heard of.

So as this cheeky little chappy and the company (I can't name) that he worked for had clearly taken us all for a little ride and he was simply making it all up as he went along, we did what anyone in our circumstances would do....

We waited until he went to sleep....

Raided his tent....

And then used all of his books to help keep the fire alight while we finished off the rest of the alcohol!

Chapter Nineteen

The Gentle Touch

The husband's entry

So I grabbed a man's bum today.

As you do!

Not just a light, accidental, get away with it kind of brush with the back of my hand when I passed either.

No.

A full on, slap him right on the cheeks, arse grab.

And not even someone I knew either.

As if that would make it any better.

No, I literally grabbed a complete stranger's arse in a beer garden in front of everyone and then stared him in the eyes as he glared down at me.

Luckily for me he had a tray of drinks in both hands otherwise I'm fairly sure this chapter would be going in a completely different direction, however that damn tray of drinks was the cause of the problem.

You see, I'd been invited to meet up with a friend at a local hotel he was staying at not far from where I live.

He was there for the weekend with his wife to very soon be and both their families and he wanted to meet up.

And it was a rather posh hotel as well.

With rather posh residents.

And certainly not the type of residents that looked like they might go for that *'man on man slapping on the arse'* kind of playful fun either.

And being the height of summer and not managing to find my friend in the hotel bar I proceeded to venture outside... following behind a slow moving middle aged, capable of handling himself, resident carrying a silver tray full of drinks he had just purchased at the bar.

I was in no rush and if I'm being honest, was actually grateful of the snail pace as it gave me time to scan my surroundings in the hope that I could spot my friend and then maintaining the same pace, casually stroll over all confident and cool like to join him without having to do that awkward thing when you are on your own and looking for someone in a crowded bar that involves you having to literally walk up to groups of people that you don't know as you hunt for that person you're meeting up with looking like the weird guy who's come out drinking on his own again and has no mates and is desperately looking for someone, or even a group of people, that might make just enough eye contact that he could then be in with for the rest of the night.

Trust me, I've been on the other end of that scenario enough times to know how irritating it is and when, like me, you don't have the backbone to say *'sorry mate, would you mind terribly just pissing off'* you end up stuck talking to them all night.

For example....

It was the last night of our friend's holiday -- they we're leaving the resort early the next day and me and the wife still had a few days left, so I headed over to the all inclusive bar to get our *'last night together'* drinks in before we all retired to bed.

So I order our final round of all inclusive drinks and in doing so some loner doing the *'leaning on the bar on one elbow while sipping his all inclusive cocktail and scanning the room for either someone to chat to or someone to chat up pose'* engages me with the universal greeting that goes something like... *'alright!'*

In an American accent.

I throw a casual glance his way along with a smile and casually return with something like *'good thanks!'*

Something like that.

What I'm fairly sure I didn't say to him was *'thank God you've spotted me mate, I was looking for a way to get out of the last drink with my dear friends who I won't be seeing again for some time as they live a few hundred miles away from me and despite the fact that you can obviously see I'm ordering four drinks and although I am British, surely even you can't possibly mistake me as being the kind of person that is likely to order four of the most obscure cocktails from the list to neck down all by myself... so please keep talking to me.'*

Because he did.

Four about forty five minutes.

And I couldn't get away from him.

And believe me I tried.

Telling me that he used to be a fighter pilot and now was an airline pilot and he hates his job but one of the perks is that he gets put up here and he loves it because there's a free bar and he can get completely pissed and not spend a penny while chatting up all the women who stay here.

And he clearly was completely pissed.

And on his own.

Which means that the rest of his crew had either abandoned him a long time ago or didn't want to spend any time with him.

And I could see why.

"So when are you flying next?" I innocently enquired, half expecting him to say 'oh, in a few days'.

"First thing tomorrow morning."

"So, (daft question I know but...) won't you be over the limit?" I gestured at the rather impressive collection of empty glasses that surrounded him.

And I know from my pilot friends that the drink / flying limit is even less than the drink / driving limit.

"Ah... I'll just go for a run in the morning!"

BRILLIANT!

And all just so casual like.

That'll be perfectly fine then -- and be sure to tell all the two hundred passengers who are putting their delicate lives in your hands that as well.

'Ladies and gentlemen, this is your captain speaking... we will shortly be taking off on our heading for wherever it is we're going oh and by the way I sunk way too many cocktails at the free bar last night and so am probably still over the legal limit but not to worry because I've done a run this morning!'

I've had those nights before now and believe me, the only run I've managed to do is to the toilet.

And in the end my wife had to come over to rescue me and can you believe he actually started chatting her up.

It's true.

Although she, as with most women, is quite used to that and so hit him back with one of her standard replies and dragged me away from him.

Which is what I should have done.

Mental note -- think up some standard replies for all possible future situations.

By which time our friends were heading off to bed.

So I didn't want to be *that* guy and as I was scanning the outside area as quickly as I could, the paper receipt from his drink tray caught the wind and blew off.

And then I, being the good kind of samaritan that I am, and just reacting (and not thinking) attempted to grab it before it hit the floor and it just so happened that by the time I had focussed on the position of the receipt as it floated to the ground and made my grab for it, it was level with the guys backside and at that point I should have thought 'LEAVE IT!' but of course I didn't as I was already fully committed however in that millisecond as my hand moved forwards for it did manage to think *'don't attempt to grab it as in doing so I would end up closing my fist and consequently punching him on the arse'* and far better (*far better?!!!*) to stop it using the open palm, slap and pin technique instead.

On his arse!

I slapped a complete stranger on his arse.

And for a very brief moment, he looked round with the start of a smile forming as he naturally expected to then see someone he knew.

Possibly his wife, who may well have given him a cheeky slap on the bum had she sneaked up behind him, but oh no....

He saw me!

Once he clocked my *'oh shit, what have I just done'* face staring back up at him with a nervous *'he's going to kick the shit out of me now, how do I explain this'* smile, he stopped dead in his tracks, almost spilling his tray of drinks everywhere in disbelief and said "*what the HELL are you doing?!*"

And rightly so!

I would have done the same.

And from my embarrassed, half squat, hand *still* on his arse (well, I didn't want the receipt to blow away) position, I simply said....

"Err... you dropped your receipt!!

And then proceeded, still in my half squat position, to reveal said receipt unto him.

Well I thought I had got away with it as he just shook his head and kept walking, however I only had time to stand upright and take a deep breath as I then make eye contact with my friend, his wife to soon be and ALL their family members, who stare at me in disbelief and greet me not with the standard greeting that you would expect from a friend you hadn't seen for a while but instead with... "*do you know him?*"

BRILLIANT -- they all saw it!

"You mean the guy whose arse I just slapped?"

"Yeah."

"No, never met him before in my life."

So my friend's good lady wife to soon be, his family, and hers, none of which I'd ever met before, now thinks he has a pervert for a mate that gets his kicks from touching up strange men in posh hotels.

And needless to say they haven't replied to any of my e-mails since.

And I can't really blame them.

After all.

And from *all* my past experiences.

I know only too well....

You never really get a second chance to make a first impression!

Chapter Twenty

Toilet Training

The wife's entry

"I smell like my Grandad!"

These were the quite *'matter of fact'* words that left the mouth of my husband as he stood in front of the bathroom mirror trimming his nose hair.

I don't know what was more disconcerting.

The fact that he actually articulated those thoughts into words.

And possible even for my benefit.

Or....

That fact that I had just walked in on him as he stood there in his underpants desperately trying to ram his electric shaver as far up his nasal passage as he could.

"What the hell are you doing?!"

"Stray nose hair."

Again... so matter of fact.

The bizarreness of it, just rolling off his tongue.

Where had the mystery gone I wondered as I backed out of there very slowly, trying not to make eye contact.

I remember the days.

Those good old days, when things were still fresh in our relationship.

Still new.

We were continuously finding new things out about each other.

Exciting things.

What's your favourite band?

What food do you like to eat?

What do you look for in a relationship?

Y'know, those all important *'can I see myself spending the rest of my life with this person or are they just a psycho?'* kind of questions.

Those were the exciting times.

The days before he'd think that there was absolutely nothing wrong with leaving the bathroom door open as he took care of *'what came naturally'*.

I could *almost* forgive him when we moved into our first house together as it was small and thus only had one toilet and bathroom combo, so if I happen to walk in on him, it was sort of my fault.

Although he could have just locked the bloody door.

But once the man in your life thinks it's okay to break wind in front of you and make no attempt at all to even acknowledge it, let alone apologise… you know it's downhill from there on.

Even the dog had the courtesy to glance up apologetically when it let one out as it dozed in its bed.

It would sometimes even glance round at its own backside as if its arse had taken on a life of its own.

In fact it would sometimes even leave the room.

Whether out of shame or whether even *it* couldn't stand its own smell, I'm not too sure.

But not my husband.

"Better out than in," whenever I glare angrily over at him.

So really I guess it's my own fault for letting him get away with it and equally for not saying anything the first time it happened.

In much the same way as it's probably my fault for not saying anything when I'm in the bathroom cleaning my teeth and he wanders in, phone in hand, to take care of (natural) business.

It's the only time he sends texts as well.

And sometimes he sends a LOT of texts.

Even the kid's are wise to it now.

My phone will bleep as I'm driving and my daughter will grab it and announce... *"It's a text from daddy. He must be having a poo."*

So, after much discussion, the declaration that my husband thinks he smells like his Grandad isn't actually anything I feel I need to concern myself with as it turns out that it's not actually him that smells like his granddad... but his shaver.

And I guess it probably would do when it's shoved half way up his nose.

But then that does beg the question *'what the hell did his Grandad used to smell like?'*

'And why *were* you using your shaver to trim your nose hair?'

Apparently the nose trimmer I bought him last Christmas had stopped working.

I guess he has a lot of nose hair grooming issues to take care of!

And while we're on the subject... me buying my husband a nose (and ear) hair trimmer wasn't because I thought that was a *really* caring gift to get someone you love.

Or because... just what *do* you get the man that has everything.

Or even because I thought '*his ears are really getting hairier and if they carry on growing at such an alarming rate it won't be long before he resembles donkey from Shrek!*'

No!

The reason I got him a nose (and ear) hair trimmer for Christmas....

Was because he asked for one!

And I just thought '*you know what, if that's what he wants, I'm just going to go with it!*'

It's ironic isn't it that as men get older, hair starts falling out from places where it should be growing, and hair starts growing in places where it shouldn't.

He now spends more time in front of the mirror, a pair of tweezers clutched tightly in his sweaty palms, than I do.

All I hear from behind the half open door is his gasps and cries of pain as he plucks out another stray and overgrown eyebrow by its roots.

"How the hell do you women go through this, *everyday*?!"

You think that's painful... you should try child birth!

And at what point in your relationship is it acceptable to *ask* someone to get you a nose hair trimmer for Christmas?

Is it at *that* point.

The point where there's really nothing left to learn about each other?

Nothing left to find out.

You know it all.

Either by asking.

By discovery.

Or worst of all....

By accident!

Thankfully he had asked *me* to buy it for him and no one else.

He's a difficult person to buy for at the best of times, as I guess, most men are, particularly as he doesn't ever give it any thought and then, when people just go out and buy him something that they think he might like, he just moans about it because of course, it's never what he wanted.

He did once, and I'm not making this up, ask my sister to get him some pants.

In his defence, it was an innocent answer to an equally innocent question.

However, my sister, who is happily married, didn't quite feel it was her place to get my husband pants, so politely declined.

And got him a book instead.

THANK GOD!

So now I simply let the kids choose his Christmas pants for him, which they think is great.

There were *'Toy Story'* pants last year.

'Power Rangers' the year before that.

And he does wear them.

Mainly when they're the only ones left and he can't be bothered to make the small trip from our bedroom across the landing to the airing cupboard to check if there are any others in there that are dry.

I really hope he never gets hit by a bus.

Even my son, aged ten, wears Calvin Klein's.

But then again he's quite the trendy little man.

It's like they've swapped roles.

He woke up one morning and said he wanted to start styling his hair (my son that is, NOT my husband -- as he doesn't have that much hair left to style), which I have to say was a relief because prior to this he'd just wake up, hair everywhere like that guy in the TV ad where the Gorilla drags him around the bedroom all night, and then just head off to school.

And I'd try to get him to at least flatten his hair down a bit before he left the house in the morning so he didn't look quite so ridiculous, but he'd kick off so much that it was an easier life for me if I simply kept quiet and dropped him off a street away instead.

And so I now find 'hair stuff' handwritten in a ten year old boy's handwriting, at the bottom of my shopping list.

And so that's yet *another* thing I have to take care of on my weekly supermarket shopping spree.

And how many different types of hair products are there for men?

Gel.

Wax.

Clay.

Putty.

Cream.

Paste.

Oh my God!

I stood there for about half an hour reading the backs of each one, trying desperately to understand which one does what... and then just gave up, closed my eyes and grabbed one.

So every morning now he hogs the bathroom mirror for about twenty minutes, styling and re-styling his hair ready for school.

And then no sooner has he got it looking just right, he slaps a bike helmet on and ruins it all.

Luckily there are no mirrors at his school (which I find strange) and so a simple *'yep, still looking good'* seems to suffice when he finally arrives at the other end resembling Bob Geldof on a bad hair day.

So if he's not shoving electric devices into orifices that they're not supposed to be shoved into and claiming he smells like a seventy five year old man, he's trying his hardest to act like one.

We live on a bit of a mixed housing estate.

We're probably the youngest of all its residents.

The houses opposite us contain *'the retired'*.

Inhabitants that have served their time and are now happily spending what's left of it out in the garden.

And so consequently their gardens resemble the Chelsea Flower Show, all year round.

Lawns that the *'Crown Green Bowling Association'* would be happy to hold a tournament on.

Our lawn however....

We'll, did you ever see that episode of the X-Files where the two main characters, I don't know their names, the women hasn't really done much else and he's been in a few things that I didn't think were very good either, well one episode that I was forced to sit through involved them moving into a house on this, way to friendly housing estate, where every house and garden (purposefully) looked identical but if a newbie moved in and changed something to do with their house or garden, and thus changed the cosmetics of the street, they mysteriously disappeared with no trace.

Well that's kind of where we live.

And our garden has gone rapidly downhill since we moved in.

We have a lawn that looks less like a tennis court and more like it's got a touch of mange.

And so needless to say we're not going to win the 'Estate of the Year' award -- again.

And neither are we going to win 'The Most Popular Family On The Estate' award either.

It's not that my husband doesn't like gardening.

He HATES it!

"It's for old people... like that lot opposite!"

He did try his hand at gardening once though to give him his credit.

A close friend of his runs his own gardening business back up north and is very successful and I think hanging around with him for all those years, well something had to rub off -- momentarily at least.

The house we first moved into had a very small rear garden but its previous owners clearly didn't care that much about it as it was in a bit of a state.

So, my husband, being the budding Alan Titchmarsh that he is (was) decided to spruce it up a bit but, and as you well know, he's also a tad '*careful*' with his money (tight arse) and therefore wouldn't actually *buy* any new plants or flowers.

No.

Instead, he thought he could make the garden look a bit more presentable, and on the cheap, by simply *moving* some of the existing flowers around a bit to create bunches, or areas, of flowers (like a flower bed) instead of having the odd flower growing randomly here and there and really looking out of place.

And so he did.

But, he was careful not to overdo it, and by that I mean, overdo the work and not the garden… so he simply did it in stages.

Very small stages.

He took some perfectly happy flowers, dug them up and moved them to another section where he thought they'd look much nicer.

They died.

So he tried again with some more perfectly healthy flowers.

They died.

Not to be outdone by nature he tried again.

And by this time, I hasten to add, he was on his own as my suggestion of simply going and actually buying or even… getting some expert advice, was met with its usual condemnation that I have become so familiar with when I suggest we (he) spends some money.

He took a bunch of bright yellow flowers and moved them to where another group of the same bright yellow flowers were flourishing.

And as proud as punch he gleefully informed me that '*this time they didn't die.'*

And apparently a few days later they *still* hadn't died.

So apparently he'd cracked it.

And oh my God, was I about to eat some humble pie!

By the time he had finished, all we had left in the garden were these bright yellow flowers and, as he didn't want to have to spend any money, he took great care of them.

He'd be out there morning, noon and night... watering them.

He even went out and bought plant food from the local garden centre.

I know, I know -- spending money.

Even I couldn't believe it.

And he'd feed and water them twice, sometimes three times a day.

And they flourished.

More and more of these yellow plants started to grow.

Within an incredibly short space of time the whole garden was array with these yellow flowers.

Nothing else.

Everything else he'd tried moving around had died.

But somehow he had managed to cultivate these bright yellow flowers.

He'd even sit out on the garden on an evening, a cold beer in one hand, and admire the garden.

He was happy!

And therefore I was happy (indoors reading my newspapers -- well the garden was now *his* thing and I was equally happy to leave it as his thing!).

And naturally before long, his friend came to stay with us.

And my husband was so excited.

Not because the long time friend that he hadn't seen for ages was finally coming to stay and they had so much to catch up on.

No.

Because his long term friend was a gardener and would no doubt be dead impressed that he had now become quite the gardener himself.

"You never know, he might even ask me for some tips!"

Could you just imagine!

Now my husband loves to show off but, and I have to say, he's not the kind of person that will show off obviously... at first.

He's more the kind of person that will put you in a position where *you* start the conversation moving and he then takes over and just won't shut up.

And so you leave.

A bit like having pre-dinner drinks in a newly decorated lounge -- that kind of thing.

So his friend arrived on the doorstep and before he'd even had time to get his overnight bag out of the boot of his car my husband had him sat down in the garden, a cold beer in tow.

"This is a nice little garden isn't it?"

"Oh... do you think so?"

His friend nods and takes another innocent sip from his bottle.

"Yeah, I've become quite a dab hand at gardening. To be honest there's not that much to it really is there? You just have to become one with nature and then things just start happening for you. It's like, if you respect nature, nature respects you."

OH MY GOD!

"It's funny isn't it but if you think about it you literally have the power to create life. Or even destroy it. In your hands. Y'know like... like a God almost!"

That's it... I get up and start heading back inside.

And naturally my husband is too caught up in his prepared speech to even notice.

"Well you've done a pretty good job."

I'm out of there.

"It's just a shame about one thing...."

I stop dead in my tracks.

So does my husband.

"Really? What's that?"

I slowly turn round so I can yet again, catch that momentary look on my husband's face.

That momentary look just before he's able to take back control of his emotions and the contours of his face give away what's really going through his mind at that exact moment in time.

This is going to be fun!

And so it was that my husband....

The gardening expert....

The modern day Percy Thrower....

God's gift to the gardening fraternity!

For the past few months….

Had actually been cultivating… WEEDS!

Chapter Twenty One

The Collectables

The husband's entry

Here's a question for you....

If time travel is going to be invented at some point in the distant future, don't you think we'd know about it by now?

My son is obsessed with time travel, which I think has a lot to do with *'Doctor Who'* which he's also obsessed about.

Doctor Who was one of those moments in his life, a little bit like him setting up an e-mail account (remember that chapter?), when *apparently* everyone in his school was watching it except him and, us being the mean and fun ruining parents that we are, meant that it was really unfair because he was missing out on all the in depth playground discussions that inevitably took place on a Monday morning.

At a first school!

I remember watching Doctor Who as a kid back in the seventies and to be honest... it terrified me.

As I think it did most kids back then.

And I can't remember if it had an age rating slapped on it.

Or if it was on after the watershed.

But parents back then... particularly mine, were a little more liberal and so I was allowed to watch it.

And I was literally one of those kids that either had to hide behind the sofa and with the lounge door wide open.

I really did!

Or I had to make sure that both my parents, the dog, the cat and the goldfish (in its bowl) were all sitting on the sofa watching it with me.

I remember watching *'Alien'* for the very first time as a teenager.

I was in the house all alone and proceeded to watch it with the front door wide open and with me standing in the lounge doorway so I had a clear line of site and sprint free access to the outdoor world -- just in case.

Just in case WHAT?!

Because statistically speaking, I was more likely to have had some serial killer type person storm into the house and brutally murder me, especially with the front door being wide open, than some fictional, make believe, alien creature hiding somewhere in my house.

And why do we think that the only time we're likely to be attacked by someone or something is when we're watching a horror film?

Like the thing that's causing all the horror waits for you to put the film on and then that's its cue to jump out on you as well.

I don't watch a comedy and then think *'I need the loo so better put all the lights on in the house and take my mobile with me with 999 already punched into the keypad as my finger hovers over the SEND button, just in case'* yet I do when I watch a horror film.

I remember on one occasion, sitting right in front of the TV, glued to Doctor Who (guess there wasn't enough room for me on the sofa with the rest of the family members who had been forced to watch it with me) safe in the knowledge that my parents were sat within *'jumping on the lap'* distance behind me and when it finished looking round only to find that they had both sneaked out of the lounge and I was in fact in the room all alone and had been for pretty much the whole time.

Sneaky little parents of mine.

But that's how scary Doctor Who used to be.

I literally couldn't take my eyes off the screen.

Which probably explains a lot now!

So remembering this, and I have to say, we are the kind of parents that won't let our ten year old watch a fifteen certificate movie, much to the frustration of our ten year old.

'It's *fifteen* for a reason!'

He still doesn't get it.

In fact thanks to the joys of *'shut your Facebook'* I often get *'informed'* how one of our friend's ten year old kids (who shouldn't be on Facebook anyway) has just won a *'trophy'* playing something like *'Call of Duty -- Advanced Warfare'*, which, as we all know, is an eighteen -- and even if it wasn't... even if somehow a parent had had a momentary lapse of judgement or even given in to peer pressure and overlooked the huge red, in your face '18' symbol slapped on the front of the box, then surely just the name would somewhat indicate the nature of what they were about to unleash on their child and NOT buy it for them, let alone let them actually play it.

Anyway, remembering how scary I used to find Doctor Who back in the seventies when, if you watch one of those same episodes now, you realise it was actually really shit, I made the judgement call of suggesting that perhaps he should stick to *'Ben 10'* but as is always the case, his constant winging eventually got the better of me and, mainly because I thought *'right, sod it, watch one and then perhaps you'll realise just how scary it is and maybe afterwards won't want to watch another'*.

And he knows that constantly winging ply will work with me.

And I know he knows.

And yet he still does it.

And it works!

It's a bit like the time he wanted to get Boris, his lizard and he went on and on and on about it, promising that he'd spend all his pocket money on crickets and that he would look after him and clean him out each week and just three months later I'm the one cleaning him out as my son sits crossed legged next to me reading a book and I'm up to my elbows in sand, dried kale and cricket shit.

Or the time he went on and on about getting a remote control helicopter and played it to death for all of a day and now neither he nor I could tell you where the damn remote control for it is.

Or all of the useless crap that we used to buy for him when he was quite new and we thought that saying no to him when he was in a shop would dramatically scar him in years to come and that clearly he did really, *really* want that particular toy but in actual fact it wasn't that he wanted that thing in particular but that it was just shiny and in fact if the shop had attached some flashing lights to a sheet of silver foil and put that on a toy shelf with a price ticket next to it he'd have also wanted that.

And all the other things that we've either bought him or endured over the years that despite knowing at the time they would turn out to be a waste of money and sure enough I was right, I still bought them for him.

To the best of my recollection it went something like....

Trash Packs
Those stupid garbage characters that the kids collect and swap and then if you haven't wasted enough money you can also buy add ons for them like garbage vans and garbage cans and even whole garbage towns.

And I don't even really know what the point of collecting them was as he and his mates didn't so much collect them to build up a set but more, passed them all around one another as he'd get one, be over the moon about it, especially if it was a rare one, then to my disbelief swap it for another one, then swap that for another one and then end up back with the original one.

But not the original one in mint condition.

258

Oh no!

The original one that looked like it had actually spent three weeks in the trash as by the time he got it back it looked like it had been used as an eraser, got lost behind the fridge and finally wrenched out of the slobbering jaws of a rabid dog.

He (I) spent a fortune on them only for the craze to suddenly change literally overnight to....

Moshi Monsters
Now thankfully this one was a little cheaper as you could play this for free.

However his mates didn't play for free (of course they didn't), so we had to stump up five pounds a month for a subscription for a game that you *could* play for free but apparently that wasn't the way you played it.

To be honest, I really couldn't get my head around that one!

And not satisfied with charging kids a fiver a month to play a game that they could also play for free, the game designers also launched stickers that you could also collect and stick BLOODY EVERYWHERE that I then had to spend hours scratching off.

I gave up in the end and had to advertise all the stuff he'd grown out of on eBay with the added description '... *complete with Moshi Monster stickers*!'

Then that craze morphed into....

Club penguins
Which was just as mad and pretty much the same as Moshi Monsters and to be honest, other than different characters, I still don't get what was so popular about it.

You created a penguin (a PENGUIN!) and then you and your mates could all meet up in a virtual world and hang out together.

As PENGUINS!

Just reading that back to myself makes it sound all the more weird.

As well as totally wrong!

That's the problem with society today.

Why can't kids just hang out with each other?

And at someone's house.

Why do they think it's cool to create an avatar of themselves.

Name it something daft like 'Rooneyisthegreatest247'.

And then just bum around on a computer screen for hours.

And not even able to talk to each other either.

They could type out messages but as he and his mates couldn't actually write back then he may as well have mashed his palm all over the keyboard for all the sense his nonsensical writing made.

I remember setting up my Playstation for online gaming and me and my mate (who was at his house in another part of town) hooking up in a gaming zone and instead of discussing strategy and game plan with the rest of our team and through our headsets using the internet (for free), instead passing those headsets over to our other halves and thus drastically reducing the phone bill!

Always thinking you see!

So there was me and my middle-aged mate along with twenty teenage gamers that we didn't know, all about to storm a building and kill the terrorists and our twenty team mates are there discussing tactics and battle plans and there, on the other end of the mic, are two mad housewives, who they can only assume *must* be playing the game with them, talking about handbags and shopping.

Which they must have figured was probably the reason why those two characters were always getting killed off within seconds of the game starting.

If only they knew the truth!

And is also probably the reason our fifteen year old team mates blocked us from ever joining their team again.

And from there we had....

Skylanders
BRILLIANT!

What a truly brilliant piece of marketing that was (and still is)!

Bring out a video game that requires you to buy additional plastic characters in order to play it and of course charge the bloody earth for them as well, and you're on your way to a fortune.

Rumour had it that one of the kids at his school had the whole set and so begins the very expensive and pointless obsession.

Every Saturday we had to head down to the local Tesco's to spend hours looking at all the different Skylander characters and look... because at seven, eight, nine and even ten pounds a pop, I certainly wasn't buying any.

Christmas and birthday's were easy though as you just simply handed out a photocopied piece of paper consisting of all the names of the Skylander characters with the ones he already had crossed off.

And of course the game couldn't be fully completed unless you had all the right characters, so this too encouraged our son to badger his poor old parents (us) into spending even more money on them for him.

And once the game was complete, which naturally didn't take all that long, the makers of Skylanders, very clever people they are, brought out *another* game... which was very kind of them.

But of course you couldn't just use the same characters that you'd already spent a small fortune on.

Well, no that's not fair... you could, but you just wouldn't get very far.

So instead you had to buy a whole new set of characters that cost twice as much as the last lot as these new ones were completely different, given a new, cooler name, and were (just a little bit) bigger.

And so it started again.

In fact this fad lasted quite a while and cost us a fortune.

And you couldn't simply swap characters with your mates for ones that you'd played with as each character was specially programmed to save information about itself so if you lent it to someone and that person 'formatted' it, you'd then have to start all over again to build that character back up again.

And just when you'd spent the equivalent of a small family holiday on collecting all of the latest set of characters, those kind and considerate makers of Skylanders launch yet another game.

And this time guess what?

That's right... you had to buy a whole load of new characters.

And then bloody Disney got in on the act, so in the end I promised I'd put away the same amount as I was spending on Skylander characters each month to save for a car for him and thankfully that did it.

And he then moved on to....

Rubbers
Yes, you read that right....

RUBBERS!

Those things that you can use to rub things out.

And not just *'normal'* rubbers of course.

No....

Fancy rubbers that you *can't* use to rub things out as you'll wear them out.

Or in the case of my kids... have nicked.

And by now my daughter has got involved as you can get some really girly rubbers and so it costs me twice as much.

And the trash pack mentality starts up again.

Buy a rubber, give it away or swap it.

Then regret giving it away and get upset about it.

And then ask your parents to speak to the parent of the kid they gave it away to and ask for it back.

Yes that's right... we really did have to approach some kid's mom in the school playground and ask if they could get the rubber back from their kid so I could give it back to mine.

RUBBERS!

There were rubber fights in the classroom.

But how do you ban rubbers from a classroom, especially as the kids weren't allowed to use pens.

So I think, based on the rubber craze that was sweeping the south of the country the pen manufacturers thought they'd get in on the act and brought out....

Erasable pens
Now come on pen manufacturers, these aren't new.

We had erasable pens when I was a kid back in the eighties.

And as sad as it is to admit... they were also a collectable craze back then as well.

I remember the most common ones being the yellow ones.

Everyone had a yellow erasable pen.

And then they launched a red one and everyone got one of those as well.

And then somehow, someone got a blue one and everyone went mad.

It was like they'd managed to sneak a porno mag into school and kids were desperately trying to sneak a peek at it at break time.

Rumour had it that his dad had got it from his recent trip to China, but it didn't matter as all anyone cared about was seeing it in the flesh.

I'm surprised they didn't place it in a glass cabinet in the main hall and schedule class viewing times.

Or keep it in a locked safe during break times even.

And you could also take the pens apart and swap the body with the lid and make a yellow and a red one.

And of course a red and yellow one.

And the craze of erasable pens is all well and good at my kids' school except for one small, miniscule little thing....

THEY WEREN'T ALLOWED TO USE PENS!

So that was short lived but of course in its place, just sitting there patiently waiting for its turn was....

Football
And in particular... football stickers.

My son is in to football.

And I'm not!

And to be honest, I don't *really* think my son is in to football but as all his mates are then he obviously needs to be if he's to survive his school days.

And so he keeps talking to me about football.

Mainly because he does actually know more about it than me which he thinks is just brilliant.

And also because I think he likes to try to impress me.

And I do my best to listen.

But the truth is I just start daydreaming.

"I bet you can't name all the players in the Chelsea squad Dad."

"Son, I couldn't even tell you where Chelsea is!"

And then he proceeds to recite lists of names to me which all sound foreign and could all be made up for all I know.

I picked him and his mate up from football practice the other day and all they did was chat about who they ranked as the top ten footballers in the world.

I started to reel off a few of the all time greats, you know... trying to be the cool dad.

"What about Bobby Charlton... George Best?"

And they both stared at me blankly for a few seconds and then just continued their original conversation.

Whatever happened to Kevin Keegan?

I held the lift door open for him once in a London hotel.

I think he was manager of England at the time as well.

I was in my early twenties and with a work colleague and we had both just left the hotel bar and were heading back up to our rooms and we were somewhat worse for wear and he refused to get in with us.

Funnily enough!

Probably didn't help with the pair of us shouting at the top of our voices *'look there's Kevin Keegan!'*

And then proceeding to announce *'come and join us Kev!'* as we both waved him in with drunken smiles slapped right across our stupid faces.

They both knew England did win the world cup once but neither of them have a bloody clue when and who made up the team.

In fact neither do I.

So World Cup stickers became the next craze but because England's participation in the last one was shorter than even the most disillusioned fan would have given them credit for, it was soon over.

And instead replaced with the very latest craze which is....

Match Attax
These football cards that cost a pound for about five and kids are currently spending every penny they can beg, steal or borrow on.

Forget heroin, I've found something even more addictive.

And kids are just as stupid about as well.

"Dad, I've got this weird sounding player and he's one of the hundred and also very rare. Apparently there's only three of them in the whole world. I had to swap all four hundred and sixty of my swapsies for him!"

"For *one* card! Are you serious?!"

But apparently I don't understand.

And I also don't understand when he then swaps THAT card either.

Even my daughter has gotten involved.

She thinks they're completing the album together.

Which is what he's told her.

What he hasn't told her however is that he knows all the lads in her year are still a bit daft and so as all she has to do is ask nicely and flutter her eyelashes a little they'll give her whatever she wants.

In actual fact it is *his* football album as we all find out every time she goes anywhere near it.

But fads are great.

And they are innocent.

And fun.

And they do bring people (kids) together.

Plus I'm the biggest hypocrite in the world.

I'll refuse to spend a whole pound on a sticker pack for him as it's a waste of money and then crack open a can of beer.

And at least he has something to show for his money as well.

So I eventually cave and agree to let him watch an episode of Doctor Who.

And I can't really remember much about it but there was a werewolf and it was set back in the eighteen hundreds or something and I'm very aware that the scenery looked a bit more realistic than when I last watched an episode of Doctor Who.

And like me when I was a kid he sits bolt upright and unblinking as he digests every scene.

And it ends and I say '*well, was that good?*'

And he just nods.

And then several hours later I find myself sitting up in bed with him as my wife refuses to as she's already been in to him three times already and so now it's my turn as it was me that let him watch it.

And not only that, but having already had to go through all that *'escorting him to the toilet for months on end when he was a toddler stage'* I now find myself right back there again as not only is he waking up every thirty minutes with Doctor Who related nightmares, but now won't even go to the toilet on his own, even though it being the middle of the day....

Because the werewolf might get him!

BLOODY Doctor Who!

Chapter Twenty Two

A Few Good Men

The husband's entry

So I taught my son to lie today.

At least I tried to.

I kind of figured that there is a skill to it and you're never too young to learn and now's the time he did.

And I don't feel bad about it either as kids lie all the time.

They're just really bad at it.

So I thought I'd do my bit to change all that.

And don't judge me now either because as parents we've all done it.

'Just stand on tip toe a little and you'll get on this ride... and spike your hair up a bit too!'

There's a reason there's a height restriction on a fairground ride.

See if you can guess why that it is!

'Just use the disabled toilet and if anyone says anything start limping'.

I did this once.

It's true.

I was in a pub and the main toilets were upstairs but you had to pass by the disabled toilet and the door was wide open like it was goading me in and it was empty and I just thought *'what the hell'* and when I came out, literally a few minutes later, there was an old woman in a wheelchair and someone else, possibly her middle-aged daughter, or carer even, glaring at me, so I did the only thing I could in this situation....

Smile politely at them both and then limp off.

And then had to spend the rest of my time in the pub limping everywhere in case they were watching me.

And when a friend asked me why I was limping I made up a story about pulling my calf muscle when I was out jogging the other day, which he thought was bizarre as I was walking fine before I went to the toilet.

Oh my God... a spiral of lies!

I also had to spend the whole of a sales meeting once winking at the director of the company I once worked for.

I'd never met him as I was quite new and he turned up to this sales meeting and I introduced myself to him and he winked at me.

So I winked back.

But it turns out he wasn't winking at me.

No!

It turns out he had this nervous twitch.

And so then I had to pretend I also had a very similar nervous, winking twitch as well so he didn't think I was taking the piss out of him and consequently get fired.

But I could only do it when he was looking at me as, from my fake toilet limping experience, I didn't want the rest of my (new) work colleagues to catch me winking and think that I too had a nervous twitch which I would then have to carry on for the rest of my life at the company, so I had to spend all of the sales meeting staring at my boss out of the corner of my eye and every time he looked over at me, start winking.

So not only must he have thought this weird new employee has a nervous winking twitch but that I also had boss eyes as I was constantly staring out of the corner of one of them in his direction while doing my best to also focus on the meeting speaker with the other.

For years I managed to convince my two daft kids that the burglar alarm sensors dotted around the house were actually CCTV cameras so anytime one of them did something that they then denied I would simply tell them to own up otherwise I'll go and check the camera footage and then they'll be in REAL trouble.

It never failed to work.

But then of course they got a bit older and (a little) smarter and it then worked against me as I'd say something like *'who's done this!'* in my most fatherly and authoritative way and they'd just throw me a casual glance up from their Game Boys and reply with *'go check the cameras Dad and you'll see for yourself!'* as they sit there looking all innocent.

Little buggers outsmarting me.

And now they're ten and eight and I don't know if they know those cameras aren't real and they're just playing along now but I can't use that one anymore and so we just go about our day to day business never talking about those cameras.

A bit like 'Fight Club'.

I hired a Ferrari once from one of those *'you'll never own one so do the next best thing and hire one as it's the only chance you'll ever have of sitting in it'* internet companies and I told a friend (more like an acquaintance than a friend really) it was mine.

Well, I didn't want to be the saddo that admits he hired it now do I?

In fact when I phoned up to enquire about hiring it I asked if it had any of those bumper stickers saying '**HIRE ME**!' like you see on all those limos that at first glance you think *'oh look, there must be some movie* star in that!' and then you clock the bumper sticker and seconds later the arse mooning out of the window to realise that a bunch of pissed up louts have just hired it for their mate's stag do, and the guy on the other end of the phone asked 'Why mate... do you want to pretend it's yours?!"

Well of course I do dick head.

What do you think, I'm going to pay as much to hire this for a day as I could to rent one of those converted farmhouse barns for the family for the whole week and then drive it around with a big advert on the side so everyone knows what a loser I am?

Which of course is what I did.

So I then had to pretend, every time my friend popped round, that it was in the garage... which is one massive lie as our garage is way too small to house a Ferrari unless it's a 'Matchbox' one.

Plus he could have just asked to see it... which thankfully for me he didn't.

And then as the months and now years have passed he's simply stopped asking how the Ferrari is and so now I don't know if:

1. He's just given up constantly asking to be taken for a spin in it.
2. Realises I obviously hired it... as why would you keep a Ferrari in the garage and NOT take people for joy rides in it if you owned one?

Or

3. He's just forgotten about it.

And I'm hoping it's the latter as it's now at that awkward stage in our friendship where we may both know the truth but neither of us wants to talk about it.

A bit like when you and your mate both fancy the same person.

So anyway we're on holiday and there's archery at twelve O'clock up by the main pool but you have to be twelve years old to do it and he's only ten but that's okay because being the responsible father that I am I can teach him how to beat their lie detector.

And amazingly his mum's okay with that... so let's really milk it.

"Right, so listen son, they're probably going to ask you how old you are and when they do you say twelve got it?! And now I know you are only ten and have clearly inherited your mother's side of the family's sizing genes as at ten years old you currently resemble a Hobbit and therefore don't actually look *eight* let alone ten even but take it from me, if you say it convincingly enough, they'll believe you!"

Why wouldn't they?

And it's not as if they're going to ask him for his date of birth... but just in case I got him to memorise it less two years.

And then I got him to recite it to me over and over again until it sunk in.

And then, just to be certain, I role played the whole scenario with him around the poolside.

Even throwing a few awkward questions in there like curveballs, which he handled really well.

I felt like Tom Cruise in 'A Few Good Men' prepping his witness before he stepped into the witness box.

YOU CAN'T HANDLE THE TRUTH!

And so after dealing with the daughter who also wanted to do archery and really couldn't understand that being only eight there was only so much a good, well prepared lie can do for you... we were ready!

"Hi, this is my son and he'd like to have a go at the archery you're running, if that's okay!"

Now we'd spent so much time prepping him for his first official lie that we were the last ones to arrive and all the other archers were sitting on the pre-laid out seats and there were *loads* of them.

And all of them adults.

Not one kid amongst them.

Especially no ten year olds posing as twelve year olds.

Damn!

Clearly all their fathers are way too responsible.

But that was okay as at least we could get a good look at who we were up against.

His competition if you like.

But of course now EVERYONE was staring at us and, as it was also deathly silent, they could all hear our every word.

"Okay, and how old is he?"

Brilliant!

He'd just been given his out.

He doesn't even need to lie!

I can do it for him.

"Ah, yes he's twelve… date of birth, two thousand and two."

I throw a quick, smug glance over to my wife who's just looking like we're being interviewed by the CIA for the recent bank hoist that we've just pulled off and if this all goes wrong we're likely to get thrown off the resort.

So the guy grabs a clipboard and a pen.

It worked.

FREEDOM!

I envisage that first sip of ice cold beer as I dangle my feet in the cool waters of the crystal clear swimming pool with one less kid to bother me.

Just need to get rid of the girl now and I'm home free.

For a few hours at least.

"What's your name son?"

My son tells the man his name.

I nudge my wife who maintains her icy stare, straight ahead and doesn't move a muscle.

"And how old are you?"

"I'm ten."

WHAT!

My wife just turns and walks off as fast as she can, dragging my daughter, who's now killing herself laughing, along with her.

"No... you're twelve remember!"

But it was too late.

All over.

Rumbled.

And as the guy just shakes his head at me with one of those *'do you really think you were the first to try that ploy*?!' looks, I have to silently admit defeat.

Why couldn't you be a better liar son?

Like your dad.

But to be honest, it's a lesson well learnt for him.

Crime doesn't pay.

Plus, if all else fails, I now know that my son will always have a great career as a police informant to fall back on.

Chapter Twenty Three

Sex Pest

The wife's entry

My husband lugs his bustling torso up our basement stairs, huffing and puffing like he's just gone ten rounds with Mike Tyson.

He has just gone ten rounds....

With himself though.

And a punchbag.

And with some guy that has a strange foreign accent telling him what to do from the antiquated CD player that he still owns (mainly because he's too tight to buy a new one) and that should really have gone out at the same time as the arc.

He calls it his *'home gym'*, which I think is quite sweet.

The reality is that it's just a dingy old basement with a cold, hard, stone floor, a punchbag held up by a fraying rope that's slung over a beam, the old CD player that is so old it has a cassette deck built in, much to the amusement of the kids who desperately try to cram their Ipods into it and some posters of Rocky Balboa and a few other boxers that even he doesn't know who they are but they look the part and it make his *'gym'* seem a bit more spit and sawdust, which is really only for effect and also for when his mid-lifers pop round and the gym then becomes the *'Man Cave'*.

Oh, and there's a beer fridge, naturally full of beer... and the odd energy drink -- mainly for show!

And when he's finished his monster workout (twenty minutes and then he quits before he has a heart attack), he generally lumbers up the stairs, into the kitchen and bothers me.

His usual thing is to try and give me a cuddle when he's all hot and sweaty which he knows I hate, and I know he knows I hate, but once upon a time, maybe fifteen years ago, he did it once and I must have smiled and playfully said *'get off you big lump'* and he reads that as *'honey, can you make sure that EVERY time you're dripping in man juice you come and find me and then rub it all over me please!'* like it's some perverted sexual foreplay or a scene from the pink panther where despite being told NOT to, Kato still tries to attack the bumbling Inspector Clouseau EVERY time he returns home.

And for the record, 'mankind' -- that kind of behaviour NEVER leads to the other!

Despite what the film Porky's may have you believe, women are NOT turned on by the smell of a male changing room.

Or a sweaty gym top.

I can't even stand the smell of his feet!

And while we're on the subject, and still for the record... breaking wind in front of your mates may be hilarious and help to define your friendship and at the same time clearly help to confirm your status as the dominant sex (God knows how) -- but a woman, particularly a women you are romantically involved with, will NEVER think you're a living God like you're 'mates' do, even if you can fart most of the national anthem.

In fact, here's another tip to help you understand this quite crucial point....

If your ten year old son, who's sense of humour is thus that he finds those *'comedy texting'* website utterly hilarious to the point that he nearly wets himself with laughter, and when most sane people and certainly the bulk of responsible *'mature'* adults find them completely unfunny, says to you... *'Oh Dad, that's disgusting!'* you know you've probably pushed it a little too far.

So stop!

And so the husband finally makes it to the top step without keeling over and I brace myself for his inevitable wet *'surprise'* and one that if we had a dog I would rather let it hump my right leg for half an hour if it meant not having to go through his *hilarious* ritual for the millionth time... but surprisingly, and quite out of character for him, I remain all dry.

And instead he stands there a little demur, just like the dog that has been kicked in its testicles once to often for humping right legs and has now simply given up... and he proceeds to asks me a question that I never thought I'd have the privilege of ever being asked as my reply is one that can only be given when one has been 'invited' to give it with the preceding announcement of said question.

"Honey... do I moan too much?"

Well had he not been standing directly in the firing line I would have spat my coffee all over the place.

And then, despite secretly hoping that one day the time for airing my thoughts on this subject would eventually present itself, I find myself in rather a conundrum.

One -- Do I tell him what I *really* think and perhaps hurt his big lumbering feelings?

He'll get over it!

Or two -- do I say what I *think* he would like me to say.

So I go for the third option and fire it right back at him.

"Do *you* think you moan too much?"

Clever me!

"Well it's just that I was in the car yesterday with the boy and I was chatting away while he was engrossed in his game of Star Wars Angry

Birds -- which by the way is a bloody ridiculous game, but of course I don't say that to him, and he says to me, quite out the blue... 'Dad, you moan too much!' and, well... I didn't know what to say!"

I give him one of my looks.

The look that says 'I have to agree with the boy.'

And he then proceeds to explain the situation which prompted our son's closing statement and from what I understand, and of course from his perspective, goes something like... 'he was driving down a road and there were parked cars either side of it and despite it being his right of way another car, driven by a women (what difference does that make?!), decided to drive towards him and then there was a standoff and then some cars drove up behind him and so he couldn't back up but then some more drove up behind the other car'....

And by which time I lose the will to live and when I think he's finally finished talking simply suggest that 'perhaps he should make more of a conscious effort *not* to moan as much in future.'

Well you know when you've said something you probably shouldn't have said?

Possibly brought about by not actually listening to all his moaning.

So we embark on a merry go round of 'no I'm not saying you *do* moan, no I'm not, I'm just saying....'

And so my dilemma continues.

To be honest, if he moaned any more I'd be signing him up for the re-make of that movie 'Grumpy Old Men' because that's where he's heading.

But it doesn't really matter as he then spots the post on the side and completely forgets what he was just saying and instead starts shuffling through it and realising that his beloved 'LoveFilm' DVD envelope isn't there proceeds to moan about the uselessness of the company and 'I can't believe it' and 'how bloody difficult is it to stick a DVD in an envelope, even a monkey could manage it if you trained it'....

I let him rant and rave all while silently holding up the 'LoveFilm' envelope in my right hand, sipping the coffee in my left hand and browsing through my e-mail on the Ipad -- now that's multitasking!

And all to see how long it actually takes him to notice.

About thirty seconds.

"Oh!" he replies.

I just nod and open my next e-mail.

So he rips the envelope open with the enthusiasm of a child on Christmas morning.

Pulls out the disk and announces....

'I don't believe it! Can they not get anything right? This one was on my low priority list. Look (shoving it under my nose) Oh my God... and where's that bloody CRB check, it's been five weeks now. Five days they said!'

Yes... *that* CRB check.

As his last one was so old -- about twelve years to be exact, he felt it was probably time to get a new one done otherwise people may start getting suspicious as to why he hadn't got an up-to-date one and is there something he doesn't want them to know which of course there is... he's a tight arse and doesn't want to spend the money when he knows nothing's changed!

You see that's where the CRB check is flawed isn't it?

It's only actually valid for twenty four hours.

But I guess in the defence of anyone that actually needs one, the hassle it takes to find somewhere that will do one for you (as you can't actually

281

have them done at the place that issues them which is actually a huge con as the place that issues them quotes something like *'twenty five pounds'* but say, for whatever reason, that you need to go through an *'agent'* or something, and then the agent charges you nearer to *'fifty pounds'*!) combined with the amount it costs to have it done is enough of a reason not to bother.

So he had one done through the kid's school in the end as he does some volunteering there now and again and the dear old lady that sorted it out for him and is due to retire in a few weeks, said the new system they use means he'll have it back within four to five working days.

And because it was done through the school, he can't chase it up so asked her to see if there was a problem which is causing the delay and she very helpfully informed him that from what she could see on her system, whoever carries out the checks, the police she assumes, had one last check to carry out on him and that was to see if he was a sex pest.

Well if they'd have just asked me I could have saved them going to all that trouble!

Plus he does have a criminal record!

Well, kind of....

You see he's always wanted to go to Vegas, so I thought I'd surprise him for his fortieth birthday with a five day stay at the Bellagio.

And to cut a long story short it took me ages to organise but eventually I had everything perfect and of course the best thing was I'd also managed to keep it a secret from him.

God knows how as even our dopey kids admitted recently that they've reached the age where they've started hunting for their Christmas presents.

"And where have you been looking?" I innocently enquire.

And so they proceed to openly tell me and happening to mention *'but we couldn't get up the loft'* I make a mental note to hide them all in the loft in future.

He's going to be so excited when he rips open that envelope, I thought!

And the day of his birthday inevitably arrived and I handed over his envelope with all the details inside and with much enthusiasm, and with the kids watching on, he excitedly ripped it open and pulled out my handmade invitation.

And for a very, *very* brief moment I saw a look in his eyes that, as I write this now, could have been misinterpreted for panic.

But it was very short lived, probably because he had a little audience, and so he let out the customary huge cheer, gave us all big hugs and said he couldn't wait.

And so the day arrived and we land at Las Vegas airport and make our way through to immigration and he starts acting a little nervous.

And it doesn't help that there's police and custom officers everywhere -- all with big guns.

And so I ask him if he's okay.

And he says.

And I quote.

"Um… would you be at all disappointed if you spent the next five days in Vegas… alone?"

You know when you think you know someone?

And I mean REALLY know someone!

Like, say for example, your husband of about fifteen years.

And prior to that, your boyfriend of another five.

So in total, I've known him for around twenty years.

Quite a long time really, you'd think.

Certainly long enough for him to have told me, and preferably before I had spent a small fortune on this bloody fortieth birthday surprise, that *'y'know that time when he and Mark went out to California for a week... y'know, when they were twenty two?'*

Well, apparently they hired a car.

As I knew.

And well, basically... they got a parking ticket.

And didn't pay it!'

Oh my God... for a moment there I was half expecting him to inform me that he was a serial killer, but even so, he was actually quite worried about it and *'did I think he should say something?'* as he's heard of horror stories where countries keep all this information on file and then when you enter their country again it flags up and you get arrested and thrown in a jail cell.

'Let me get my camera ready!' I thought.

So he suggests I go through the immigration check first -- just in case.

And I tell him *'not to be so daft, but okay I will'* -- just in case!

And naturally I pass straight though with no problem.

And so he steps up to the white line.

Smiles nervously at the immigration officer -- a women I'm guessing about late fifties and with a face that says *'my family have all gone out to watch the ball game today and Doris has called in sick and had I recognised the number on my phone I wouldn't have answered it but it was withheld and so here I am!'*

She just stares at him as he slides his passport over.

She looks at it.

Then at him again.

And surely even she must be asking herself the question *'why is this red faced Brit sweating all over my counter top?'*

She nods at the fingerprint scanner.

He places his sweaty little digits on the electronic device in front of him.

She hovers the 'ENTRY ALLOWED' rubber stamp over his open passport.

Stares at the computer screen in front of her.

My husband takes a big, dry mouthed gulp.

I put the camera away and pull out the camcorder now -- much better and less chance of me missing anything.

And there's clearly a delay.

Something's wrong.

And to add even more nervous tension to the situation, she actually lowers the rubber stamp and takes another long hard stare at my husband's clammy face.

And then back to the computer screen.

I half expect to see six red dots suddenly appear all over my husband's chest as he desperately tries to smile all unassumingly but instead looks more like he's suffering from piles.

And then suddenly something must have gone in his favour as she slams the stamp down hard, making him jump and hands his passport back to him along with the words *'have a nice stay!'*

"Any more secrets you're keeping from me?" I ask as he drags me VERY quickly to a waiting taxi.

And I wait until he's calmed down.

Heart rate back to normal.

Crimson cheeks back to their usual pasty white.

And drop the bombshell that could well finish him off.

"So your little parking escapade took place where?"

"Los Angeles."

"Right, right... which is California."

He nods -- although I don't think the importance of this actually sinks in.

"And we're where now?"

He looks at me quizzically... and not because he's unsure as to where we actually are, but more because he's unsure as to what I'm getting at but has at least realised that I'm building up to something and that usually when I'm building up to something in this way, it inevitably ends in either him in lots of pain, him apologising or him being slapped in the face with the big wet realisation fish.

"Vegas" he tentatively replies.

"Which is in which US state?"

Yes, that's right dear reader -- Nevada!

And as we all know, as the good old US of A is so large, it can, and often does go that things that happen in one state may well not be valid in another.

And so next year as my little treat, I'm planning on taking all of us to Disneyland.

Not the big one in Florida however.

No!

The smaller one that is located in Anaheim.

Anaheim....

CALIFORNIA!

And I'll be sure to take the camcorder with me there as well!

Chapter Twenty Four

The Perfect Crime

The husband's entry

So it's winter, which means one thing in our household….

'The Battle For The Thermostat'.

It sounds like the title of a really bad Hollywood movie doesn't it?

But I can assure you it's not.

In fact it's even bigger than any Hollywood blockbuster!

You see my wife and I have different perspectives when it comes to heating control.

I like to adopt more of a Mediterranean approach to having the heating on -- which is basically… I don't.

Whereas my wife, on the other hand, seems to think we're living in the North Pole and consequently has it on FULL blast all day.

And all night!

I don't know whether this attitude stems from my childhood when money was a lot tighter and so anytime I'd happen to mention to my mother that it was so cold in my bedroom the window was frozen up again (on the inside) and could she possibly see to it that the thermostat went up a degree (so from ten to eleven) as it was clearly bloody freezing, and she would simply tell me to go and stick another jumper on and man up.

The thing is, I already had eight jumpers on and literally couldn't fit another one on top and still hope to be able to move my arms or get through any of the doors even.

Or her other standard response was *'if you want the heating turned up, go and get a job and then you can pay the fuel bills and have the heating on as much as you want.'*

You know it's pretty cold indoors when you go *outside* in the thick of winter and have to take layers off as you're too hot!

I remember she once refused to let me use the home telephone when I hit the age where, despite spending all day at school with your mates, and also despite the fact that you were going to see them again once you'd got changed out of your lame school uniform, you still had to phone them the minute you got in to make sure none of them had died in between arriving home, doing homework or eating tea.

And because she couldn't trust that I *wouldn't* use the phone and run up her bills for her, she actually unplugged it.

And then hid it.

So I did the only thing a teenage boy with a part time paper round could do when one finds oneself in that situation....

I bought a cheap one from Dixons and used that to call them on when she wasn't around.

But I also stupidly threw the receipt for it in the bin.

And she found it.

And then demanded I hand the phone over.

And so that was that!

Foiled again!

The only time the heating went up to any respectable level in our household was when my father came home, which wasn't very often as he was either at work all day or in the social club all night -- which I think was because it was so bloody cold in our house he didn't want to come home.

And I can't blame him.

But I do believe that having to deal with the cold all the time makes you a bit hardier to it.

At least that's what I keep telling my wife.

However the truth is that I have clearly inherited my mother's tight arse genes.

I remember in my teens my mother would head off to work in the local village pub on a Friday night leaving me to look after my younger sister and although we did have a gas fire in our lounge, it was mainly just for show as it never went on.

Well actually that's not entirely true as I do remember it did used to get switched on but only really so my mother could hang wet washing in front of it when it was raining outside.

Well I remember owning a pair of brown cords (it was the seventies remember) and they had been washed and were damp and as I really wanted to wear them on one such occasion I asked my mother if I could put them in front of the fire to help dry them quicker.

As the fire was on and already drying washing she naturally agreed so being a young, I don't know, maybe seven year old, naïve (which is really the politically correct way of saying 'stupid') kid I laid them out on top of the fire.

Yes that's right -- ON TOP of the gas fire, so that the legs of them literally dropped down in front of the flames.

In fact the only thing stopping the legs from sitting *in* the flames were the thin wire protective bars on the front of it.

And then I plodded back in to the kitchen to eat my tea.

And within a few minutes we started to smell smoke, which we just assumed was the neighbour having yet another *'burn all the evidence'* bonfire.

And as we had one of those hatchways between the kitchen and the living room, a few minutes after smelling smoke... we also started *seeing* smoke.

And I just remember my mother literally dropping everything, sprinting into the lounge and screaming, with me following close behind her, to witness my brown cords completely engulfed in flames, along with the seventies shag pile carpet as flaming pieces of my trousers had dropped onto it and set it alight and the room completely full of smoke.

As was most of the house by now.

Anyway, none of us died that day (obviously), and once we'd gotten a rug to cover the fire burns on the carpet, and had the lounge and ceiling redecorated, the curtains replaced, furniture rearranged so you couldn't see the charring on any of it, and everything fumigated... you'd have hardly of noticed.

And so that was the end of the fire being on when the kids (mainly me) were awake.

So, my mother would head off to the pub and within a few minutes of her walking out the door and me ensuring my sister was safely tucked up in bed, as she would have snitched on me the next day, it went on FULL BLAST!

In fact it was so bloody hot that I had to have all the doors and windows open at the same time.

Never really occurred to me to simply turn it down.

But it was lovely.

Heat at last!

And naturally I'd switch it all off before heading off to bed so she'd be none the wiser when she arrived back home again.

The perfect plan!

And then I'd get up the next morning, wander downstairs and straight into the kitchen and the icy glare of my mother.

"Had the fire on last night did you?!"

"What? No!"

My perfect plan flawed by the fact that she was also too tight to pay for decent loft insulation and consequently we were the only house in the street at half past midnight (when she drove back home) that had a perfectly, frost free roof!

Who else would have even noticed that?!

Plus, it must have been like a bloody sauna as she walked in, which I also never accounted for.

So that was the end of my little tropical Friday nights!

But what was I thinking really?

Even if I had gotten away with it, it would have all come out when the gas bill came in the following month.

I remember going swimming once with my mates in the local swimming baths when I was around about thirteen years old.

I wasn't actually allowed to go swimming with my mates for whatever reason.

I think she thought that I was that daft I'd probably drown myself.

But nevertheless, all my mates were going swimming -- again, and I wasn't missing out this time.

And when I arrived back home I did that thing that I had seen my mother do a hundred times before, which was to rinse the chlorine out of my trunks in the bathroom sink before putting them in the wash basket.

Perfectly plausible I thought and clearly the done thing, so I followed suit.

Only... instead, I put them back in my pants drawer where they lived.

Genius... because if she'd have seen them in the wash she would have instantly known I'd been swimming as even I didn't think I could get away with saying I'd worn them in the bath.

How was I to know she had plans to take us round to her friend's house the very next day who also had kids *and* a paddling pool?

It's true!

So my perfect plan was foiled again owing to me doing the right thing after doing the wrong thing.

And of course her discovery of my still wet budgie smugglers.

She would have made a great detective as she managed to solve all my crimes in record time!

But then again my downfall was that I was clearly a very *conscientious* teenage criminal.

I'd have probably been the kind of burglar to vacuum up any mess I made so at least the owners came back to a nice tidy house.

"As you can see officer, the TV's been nicked but at least he's polished the sideboards!"

I remember once, as a very young kid, probably around the age of five or something, hating corned beef sandwiches, and unfortunately for me corned beef was very popular where I grew up.

And also very cheap.

And there was a reason that it was so cheap….

Because it tasted like shit!

And every Saturday tea time I'd be served up a plateful of corned beef sandwiches and I'd go through the same ritual of telling my mother I hated corned beef and she telling me that I still had to eat them and me refusing to and she informing me that I could sit there until I had.

And I usually did.

The same routine that now takes place in our household basically.

Only without the corned beef sandwiches.

And I'd try everything and anything I could to swallow down these corned beef sandwiches.

Holding my nose.

Taking a bite and a swig of my orange juice and chewing it all up together hoping that the orange juice would somehow disguise the taste of the corned beef… which of course it didn't, and instead I had an even nastier combination of corned beef and orange juice mix that almost made me vomit.

Or eating very small bites which took forever and was so impractical as it took just as long to get through one half of a sandwich than if I had just sat there and not eaten anything at all as I knew that eventually I would have the plate removed and be sent off to bed with no tea.

Or putting them in the bin… but of course she'd find them and then brush off the bits that had stuck to them and still make me eat them.

We didn't have a dog back then either and as I soon learnt… cats also hate corned beef sandwiches which made it even worse as I'd throw the sandwich under the table for the cat, the cat would have a good old sniff at it along with a sample, taster lick, then turn its nose up in disgust, and then I'd still have to eat it but now of course it was covered in floor dust and cat juice.

And if a cat won't eat corned beef but will happily lick its own bum all day, then that tells you just how awful corned beef tastes.

Then one day, after she had left the kitchen, I had a brainwave....

I shoved my two, uneaten, corned beef sandwich halves behind the back of our free standing cooker.

No one ever checks there!

I then waited a few minutes before wandering into the lounge all innocent like, to join my sister on the sofa just at the very start of the Saturday afternoon cartoons.

And I remember it all well.

My mother looked up somewhat surprised to see me, then asked *'have you eaten all those sandwiches?'* and I'd give her the all angelic, butter wouldn't melt in my mouth, reply of *'why of course mater, I know better than to grace you with my presence having left a few mouthfuls of uneaten corned beef sandwich resting on my dinner plate now don't I?'*

So she'd inevitably wander off into the kitchen to check and finding my plate as clean as a whistle, I'd be rewarded with a choc ice with which to sit and munch my way through all while watching said cartoons.

The perfect crime!

And one that continued on for several months.

Or at least until there suddenly started to develop a rather strange and pungent smell emanating from the kitchen area.

And neither my mother nor my father could work out what that strange smell was.

And I was so daft, I didn't put two and two together either and, along with the pair of them thought it must be a problem with the drains, which they paid good money to consequently get cleaned and it made no difference whatsoever.

Which of course it wouldn't would it?

And then eventually, when the stench had finally become so unbearable, my father decided it was time to start ripping the kitchen apart to try and find out what the hell that smell was as by now he was beginning to think the cat had brought a mouse in, it had escaped, hidden somewhere, and then died.

All I remember, and I do remember it very well, was getting called, very calmly, into the kitchen by my father, and on entering the kitchen seeing both my parents and roughly about two months worth of extremely mouldy corned beef sandwiches, all splayed out on the kitchen floor from where they had fallen once my father had pulled the cooker out... all staring back at me!

Luckily they didn't make me eat them but they might as well have done as that was that... corned bloody beef sandwiches for the entire remainder of my childhood.

Now *I'm* not so tight that I won't have the heating on.

But the problem stems from the fact that both my wife and I work from home a lot.

And in the wintertime, it does get quite cold in our house.

As it surely must do in everyone's house.

So the heating is set to come on in the morning for when we all wake up.

And in the evening when the kids are back in again.

And not a lot else in between.

That is, until my wife passes the heating controls and whacks it all back on again without me knowing.

And at first I used to think I couldn't have programmed it properly as it shouldn't be on in the middle of the day.

Particularly as my wife pretends she doesn't know *how* to switch it all back on again.

A bit like me and the washing machine!

So I'd knock it all off again.

And then I'd find it was back on several minutes later.

And then I start thinking either we have Gremlins....

I'm going mad....

Or there's something wrong with the heating system.

What I don't figure is my sneaky wife to be the culprit, as I managed to catch her in the act of switching the main controls back on again one day.

So, after about thirty minutes of me trying to explain how bloody expensive it is to have the heating on full blast throughout the whole of the winter and her simply staring at me with a look in her eyes that said *'I don't give a shit, oh and newsflash loser... I sit next to the heating controls'* I realised I was fighting a losing battle and so let her have her little victory.

But what she hadn't accounted for was that I sit close to the thermostat.

And so when she'd turn the heating back on again.

I'd turn the thermostat down to *'five'*.

And so the battle began.

And neither of us would mention anything to the other, each smugly believing that we had had the final laugh.

The upper hand, if you like.

Until it got so cold one day that even I was beginning to feel it and my wife entered my icy domain to ask if the heating was playing up as she could see it was on but the radiators were all cold.

My reply was simple.

'Put another jumper on.'

And so she did.

Plus her coat, hat, scarf, gloves and snow boots!

And she would sit there, tapping away on her laptop in her mittens (well trying to at least) looking like she was heading off on an Icelandic voyage.

But it was win, win!

She was now warm and the heating was off.

And then on one occasion I happen to wander in to see her and much to my surprise she wasn't wearing her usual arctic attire.

Instead, blasting away next to her feet was an electric fan heater.

I almost had a heart attack there and then!

"What the hell is that?!"

"It's cold!"

"Well you can pack that up for starters." I explained as I headed over to unplug it.

"Those things are even more bloody expensive than having the heating on!"

"Back away from it!" she roared.

I glanced back over to see my wife holding a pair of kitchen scissors and wearing a look on her face that said if I took another step she'd literally kill me!

"Fine, I'll turn the thermostat up!"

Oh shit!

One stupid slip of the tongue.

"What?! Is that what you've been doing? Turning the temperature down?!"

Rumbled!

And so the battle begins all over again.

She turns the heating on.

I turn the thermostat down.

She then sneaks round and turns it up.

I then sneak in and turn the heating off.

It's like some mad episode of 'Spy versus Spy' with both of us sneaking around the house, desperately trying to outdo the other without the other realising, and the one that manages to keep the heating set in their chosen position for the longest, wins.

I half expect her to wire the heating switch up to the mains.

Or I open her office door and get flattened by an anvil.

And the kids don't care.

Not only are they at school all day anyway where it's practically Caribbean temperature all year round, but despite there being seven inches of snow on the ground, kids round by us won't even wear a jumper, let alone a coat to school, as it's so un-cool.

Plus, no hat ever made is going next to my son's perfectly styled hair.

But of course there's only ever going to be one winner in all of this.

And that is....

British Gas!

As not only will we be paying them a small fortune for heating our house throughout the whole of the winter *again* this year.

But we'll also be paying them a small fortune to keep coming out to fix the bloody boiler as all that on and off, and up and down, now means we have a relatively new, three year old heating system that's already knackered!

Chapter Twenty Five

New Religion

The husband's entry

We have a simple phrase in our house that, regardless of what the kids are doing... you know -- reading, playing, studying (yeah right!), killing each other... will captivate their attention and cause them to literally drop everything, regardless of how much fun whatever it is they are currently doing may well be, even Playstation... and come running.

INSTANTLY!

And it never ceases to work.

Ever!

Sounds too good to be true doesn't it?

Well it's not!

So what is that one magical phrase I hear you ask?

Is it?

'The computer's free!'

No!

'Wait till your father get's home?!'

Like that one has ever made any difference.

'Tea's ready and it's jam sandwiches!'

Not even close!

No, the one phrase that is guaranteed to stop any riot, any expenditure of energy or whatever alternate activity that may be currently occurring in our household at that exact moment is....

'The tele's on!'

It's incredible.

Like some new age drug.

Like the kids are crack addicts and Dad's just pulled up on the drive with a fresh new batch for them.

No matter how much the kids are tearing up the house, switch on the TV and there's a sudden calm that just descends.

Over everything.

Even me and the wife.

It's like that scene in 'Wreck It Ralph' where those giant robot bugs in that videogame are unleashed and they're starting to overpower those space marines and then just when it looks like it's all over and the bugs are going to win, that beam of light illuminates the sky and they (the bugs) all stop they're rampaging and head towards it all transfixed and zombie like.

It's like that.

I read somewhere that hardcore porn played out over the big screens will instantly stop a riot at a football match.

The problem is of course they can never actually test it out for sure as the political correctness police would jump on that band wagon all day long, so far better to let them all kill each other.

But I do believe the theory.

And despite all of my arguments I think the wife may be right that I can't test *'the porn theory'* with our two kids either.

But TV is like some kind of religion in our house.

Forget Sunday worship down at the local church... the kids have made their own shrine out of the TV.

Every Sunday morning, if we don't have to be up and out of the house first thing, the kids will sit transfixed, worshipping the TV.

And often they don't even have to be interested in what's on it.

It just needs to be on, with them in the same room as it.

We turned the old nursery into a kind of kids den, complete with small TV so that on a weekend they had somewhere to go when they woke up instead of doing that old Christmas Day thing of waking up really early and then purposefully making so much bloody noise that they then wake us both up so they can open their presents.

It used to happen *every* weekend despite reading them both the riot act as we put them to bed the night before.

"Now remember kids, no noise in the morning as your mother needs her beauty sleep -- at least ten hours!"

"Yes *Dad!*"

I might as well have said....

"Now kids, make sure you wake up at least two hours earlier than you normally do on a school day morning, then creep around the house being sure to tread on every creaky floorboard you can find, particularly the one right outside our bedroom door, then whoever's up first needs to burst in to the other's bedroom to check if they're awake, discover that they are (because they'll also wake up two hours early as well), get screamed at to GET OUT! refuse, then start fighting, then knock something over and probably smash it... by which time we'll all be awake -- okay!"

Because that's pretty much what used to happen.

And then one of us would get up, mainly the wife as I pretend not to hear them, shout at the kids, then realise she's fighting a losing battle so cave in, open the stair gate (which we still have as our daughter has a tendency to sleep walk -- another long story... and I really couldn't contend with her falling down the stairs as well) , head downstairs, deactivate the burglar alarm and finally switch the lounge tele on for them to vegetate in front of till I've made their Sunday morning pancakes.

But of course then we're all awake, and have you ever tried getting back to sleep once you've spent ten minutes shouting at the kids for waking you up?!

Impossible!

Although I do have a neat little trick and one that I managed to hone throughout the whole of the *'the kids need attention'* stage during the night when they were babies.

Future fathers pay close attention!

One of them would wake and start crying which in turn would normally wake the wife and she'd be up, out of bed and into them in an instant leaving me to roll over and carry on where I had left off.

And on the odd, once in a blue moon occasion, when she was clearly so tired at having already been up several times in the night and despite that motherly gene which apparently can hone in on a child's cry (or rather scream) from three miles away, somehow she'd managed to temporarily turn it off, and then I would end up awake and clearly the only person able to deal with it so I'd inevitably do the correct and fatherly thing... elbow her in the ribs waking her instantly and then pretend to be asleep confident in the knowledge that she'd now hear the kid crying and rush off to deal with it!

And on a weekend when they *can* lay in, they're both up at six... whereas you try getting the little buggers up and ready for school in the week and that's a whole different ball game.

It would be easier to try and stop Katie Price from writing yet another autobiography!

Or appearing on Reality TV!

I don't know whether it's just a kid thing or whether it's just *our* kid thing, but it's incredible how that mind numbing, lack of thinking, big grey (flat screen -- of course) box can have more impact on the lives of our kids than we can.

Forget imparting my parental advice on them as they grow up, I'm leaving all that to the TV as I'm sure it will do a much better job than I could anyway.

And have you tried telling kids of today about TV back in the olden days?

Olden days -- I sound like my grandparents!

It's true though.

I remember the days of just three channels -- BBC1, BBC2 and ITV.

And when they launched channel four, well that was as big as the moon landing!

Although there was never anything to watch on it.

And then they launched Channel Five but they needn't have bothered as no one could actually get it... unless of course you sat your TV on top of the microwave which was running at full power with a coat hanger rammed in to the back of it attached to a huge cable of wire running the whole length of the street.

And plugged directly into Channel Five's transmitter.

And then it would probably still be just a screen full of snow.

I remember as a kid having a classroom discussion at my primary school about TV and one of the other kids said that if *they* were in charge of all the channels they'd have cartoons playing twenty four hours a day and all of us other kids gasped unanimously and agreed just how cool that would be.

And now of course it's reality and our kids just take it all for granted.

But tell a child of today how it used to be and they'll just stare at you all gormless like as if they're waiting for the punch line.

A bit like when they watch TV.

And have you ever tried watching kids TV?

I walked in on my two watching some computer generated animated trash recently and I though the TV had gone haywire.

There were flashing images, loud noises, neon colours, a thousand things all happening on screen at the same time and way too many fast cuts back and forth.

It made TIZWAS look tame!

I thought somehow the wife had slipped an ecstasy pill into my morning coffee and I was tripping.

Seriously though, I literally thought I was going to have a seizure.

But kids of today are all desensitised to it.

They've grown up with it and so can handle it.

My son, who is two years older than my daughter walks around all the time talking about his butt and instead of laughing out loud he actually says 'LOL'.

I'll do or say something mildly amusing and he won't laugh anymore, he'll literally say the word 'LOL'.

It's like TV has taken away the kids emotional genes and that's the only way they can express themselves now... by articulating it.

And it's not from texting either as he doesn't have a phone... and don't we just know about it -- which is a whole other story all in itself as well.

And my daughter's not exempt from the influences of TV either.

She knows all the words to *all* the adverts.

She can sing the whole *'Calgon'* advert word for word.

In fact it was her audition piece for our local theatre group.

My wife was wiping down the kitchen work surfaces once when my daughter was about three and sitting at the breakfast bar colouring and she asked....

"Mummy, are you using *'Cillit Bang'* for that?"

Although sadly I can still sing the *'Shake n Vac'* theme tune word for word thirty years on!

But us more *'mature'* types *can't* cope with all those flashing images.

A bit like fairground rides.

(Nice transition!)

I went to a theme park not long ago with the kids now that they're both tall enough to go on anything that doesn't involve colourful elephants going round and round (very slowly) and occasionally up and down, when the button isn't broken, and as soon as the ride took off I spent the whole time thinking I was going to die.

It was sitting next to my eight year old daughter on a rollercoaster that shot you off from standstill at something like a hundred miles an hour leaving any smug smile you may have had on your face as you sat there all cocky watching those red lights all illuminate and then finally turn green (a bit like me) back at the starting point and no sooner had you caught your breath from that you found yourself hurtling vertically upwards like a rocket and then straight back down again without warning all the time having to deal with negative this and positive that g-forces that even a skilled fighter pilot would struggle to deal with as you're literally thrown all over the place, holding down the entire contents of your stomach and putting any thoughts of, *'what happens if these restraints give out'* out of your mind.

And it's all over in about ten seconds.

And we pull back into the starting gates and my daughter, who's had her arms up the whole time, wants to do it again.

And we do.

Only because I can't get out the bloody car!

'Now you know how I feel' says my wife when I recount my *'all that build up and it's all over in ten seconds'* experience to her.

Not sure what she means by that!

But the kids loved it.

'Can we do it again! Can we do it again!'

Not on your Nelly!

But I think my new found fear of white knuckle rides is just because I'm out of practice.

No, really... I think you get used to doing something and when you do that something over and over again and don't die, you relax a little and then that's when the buzz goes.

I did a bungee jump once.

I was working at a county show back in the day.

I think it was something like *'The West Midland's Summer Spectacular'*... anyway, it was basically just a fun fair and me and my work mates found ourselves staying at the same B&B as the guys that ran the bungee jump attraction and so naturally we got talking in the bar that night and naturally, me being me, after a few beers must have made some throwaway comment like '*Bungee jumping is for wussies!*' so that was that... the next morning they came and got me and not wanting to lose face, and because I didn't want my workmates to see me squirm out of it as I'd never hear the last, I agreed to do a bungee jump.

I remember sitting in the cage having undergone check after check after check and while we were still on the ground asking if, when we reached the top, I could spit over the side onto my work mates who were all enjoying this moment a little too much.

Well, this bloody thing never stopped going up and up and up until it was so high I could probably have seen my house... had I plucked up the courage to open my eyes.

And we finally reached the top and I was given the all clear to hurl one out over the side but I couldn't move.

I was literally rooted to the spot with fear.

But not wanting to show it and of course lose face I somehow managed to hop my way over to the gate.

And held on (very) tightly as the guy opened the cage door and gave me the countdown.

THREE!

TWO!

ONE!

JUMP!

Nothing -- I froze.

JUMP!

Jump -- I couldn't even talk.

'Don't make me push you!'

"WHAT?!"

Now if you've ever done a bungee jump and haven't already blanked it from your mind you'll know exactly what I'm talking about.

Jumping, potentially to what your mind thinks is your ultimate death, is a very hard thing to do.

But I couldn't lose face.

So I took a deep breath.

Leaned over the edge.

And thinking to myself *'what's the worst that could possibly happen?'* I let go.

And I'll tell you *'what's the worst that could possibly happen...'* as I plummeted towards the ground.

I COULD DIE!

And as I gravity took over I realised, too late... I was committed.

I should have been bloody committed!

And when it was finally all over and I'd stopped doing my best impression of a human conker the bravado came rushing back.

'Yeah, well that was easy!' I announced, all cool as a cumber like and unfortunately for me within earshot of the Bungee crew.

So that was that... back up there again for a second go.

So for a short while, fairground rides were pathetic in comparison to that adrenaline rush but then I went through a stage where I didn't get to go to a theme park for quite some time -- mainly because I was no longer a teenager and so consequently had to get a job, and as a result of that you get out of the habit and then when you start getting back into the habit again you literally have to start over.

Plus, my wife claims her lack of enthusiasm now for all that white knuckle stuff has a lot to do with having kids and that in-built sense that in order to ensure they have the best upbringing that a parent can possible give them, it's probably important that you don't constantly try to kill yourself.

So as much as I hate to admit it, the only white knuckle, adrenaline rush that I'm ever really going to get now is joining my kids in front of the TV, trying desperately to get through a whole episode of whatever it is they are watching….

And all without having a stroke!

Chapter Twenty Six

Family Fun Time

The wife's entry

At least once a week, normally on a Sunday, my husband insists that we all spend some quality time together as a family.

'*Family Fun Time!*' he calls it.

Now I grant, that family life, particularly in this modern day world in which we all live, can be (and often is) somewhat hectic.

Getting the kids up in the morning, fed and out the door in time for school is a military operation in itself.

Then we have all the paperwork to contend with in order to ensure the smooth, day to day running of our family business.

And then we also have the *actual* smooth, day to day running of the business.

Along with collecting the kids from school again.

Taxiing them around to all their after school activities.

And not forgetting all the obvious stuff that goes hand in hand with running and maintaining a happy household.

While ensuring we all remain healthy.

And of course with happy kids.

And as we all know, happy kids actually involves them doing everything and anything other than spending (forced) time with their parents.

So, in order to find an hour or so for us to all participate in *'Family Fun Time!'*, we have to have a time management programme that is far superior to old Timothy Ferris and his *'4-hour working week'* philosophy.

You see my husband has these visions.

And I don't mean supernatural visions.

Like of lottery wins or earthquakes.

Or even the likes of which can be seen in those *'Final Destination'* movies.

I mean visions of how things should be.

He gets an idea to do something and then instantly pictures the most perfect scenario in his head.

Sitting around an open log fire, unwrapping presents, Christmas carols playing away in the background while snow falls all picturesque outside and somehow the dinner cooks itself... as I need to be sitting dolefully next to him sipping mulled wine (that also made itself) and smiling lovingly at him as I and the kids all thank our lucky stars to have someone as wonderful as him in our perfect little lives.

Or the four of us with huge cheery, ear to ear grins, smiling away together as we all sing, in glorious harmony *'We're all going on a summer holiday!'* as we head off in our luxurious family car to our Chav free holiday destination ready to be met outside by a greeting party with cool refreshing drinks and scented towels as we pull up, all while the sun shines, the birds sing and the M25 is accident free.

That kind of thing.

And of course, it's NEVER anything like how he pictures it will be.

In fact, if you take the most amazing and wonderful scenario for literally anything... then the complete opposite of that is what generally happens.

So of course he's always disappointed.

With everything.

So let me explain how *'Family Fun Time!'* works in our household.

'Family Fun Time!' started when our daughter was two and our son was four with a family game of Monopoly, which is the only board game we own because somehow along with my fourteen inch portable TV, stereo system complete with Wham stickers and inflatable armchair is the only other thing I managed to bring with me when we first set up home together.

In fact it's so old I think it must have originally been from my father's childhood.

Anyway, he spent thirty minutes rummaging around in the loft looking for it.

Then five minutes (approximately) cleaning it all up.

Then ten minutes (approximately) setting it up so that all four of us could play.

And it had to be all four as he also thought that introducing the kids to money and giving them the responsibility for buying and selling things at an early age would help them understand the business world better when they were older.

Of course it would -- they're two and four!

So once this is done we all get called into the dining room for his grand and very proud opening ceremony.

And from the best of my recollection I think it lasted all of about four minutes, so not even twice round the board, before the kids were bored and had both wondered off.

So all in all, he spent more time setting it all up and then breaking it all down than actually playing it.

And of course he was disappointed.

And so disappeared off into his shed to sulk.

So board games were out of the window for a few more years at least so instead he introduced the kids to *'Family Movie Time!'* because what kid doesn't love watching a good two hour long movie?

I'll tell you.

Two year old kids!

So having rented a DVD from Blockbusters (remember Blockbusters?), made us all popcorn, we were all snuggled down on the sofa together ready to watch *'The Polar Express'*, which he actually really wanted to watch, and before the opening credits had even finished scrolling up the screen our daughter had eaten all of her popcorn and was rolling around on the lounge floor.

Followed very closely by our son.

So that was that.

Back in the shed!

And so it went on.

He'd think of *'Family Fun Time!'* ideas.

I'd remind him that the kids were still only two and four.

And within ten minutes of whatever fun time things we were doing, it was generally all wrapped up. I was back to cooking the tea, the kids were back to tearing up the house and he was sawing a plank of wood in half.

In his shed.

Again!

So six years on and we all find our welcome friend, *'Family Fun Time!'* is back and this time (funnily enough) it works.

Well it works a little better at least.

So once again he's hunting up the loft for our only board game... Monopoly.

Blowing off the dust.

Polishing up the dulled metal playing pieces.

Hand writing out property cards on scrap bits of paper as we've inevitably lost even more, despite the fact that it's been sitting up the loft for six years unused.

Preparing his vision.

And sure enough *'Family Fun Time!'* kicks off and... twenty, thirty even forty minutes in and he's not in the shed yet, so I figure... it must all be going well.

But here's the thing with Monopoly.

The best selling board game of all time has one huge flaw.

It's not a game that you can all share in the experience with.

You see our son was the first one bankrupt so that was it, he was upset and of course out, and as much as I try my best to ensure my husband's visions play out, even I thought it was too much to insist he sat there watching the rest of us play the game, so he disappears up to his bedroom.

Then our *eight year old* daughter makes some *'bad business decisions'* (according to her mentor), so she's out, and heads off equally upset.

So that just leaves me and him and to be honest, I'm really not that fussed and was only really playing for the kids sake and to keep him happy, so I suggest that he's the winner, which doesn't go down well at all as he wants us to finish the game properly.

So I find myself playing a game of Monopoly with my husband, with no kids anywhere to be seen and as Monopoly is really based on the lucky roll of a dice he keeps landing on my property and for some bizarre reason I'm not landing on *any* of his, so somehow, through no intention of my own I'm winning and he's not happy and all I can think is, perhaps it's time to get him a new shed?

And so this goes on, pretty much in exactly the same way, each week, until I suggest perhaps we get a new board game.

Thankfully he thinks it's a good idea but instead of heading down to Toys 'R' Us together so we can all pick one, which thinking about it is a really bad idea as neither our son, nor our daughter can every agree on anything which is why they are no longer allowed to pick from the *Love Film Instant* movie list when it comes to '*Family Movie Time!*' (yes, that also still takes place!) as by the time they finally agree on a movie, it's time for bed, he hunts down one that he used to play when he was a kid from the only place where you can now get one....

EBay!

So we all sit round the dining room table as he explains the rules and thankfully it did come with rules as it came with very little else, as sitting on the starting square in front of us all now are:

- A Lego Ninjago figure.
- A Roman centurion helmet on a stand
- A lip balm container in the shape of a small owl.
- And Boris, the lizard -- well a smaller, plastic version of him anyway (because the real one wouldn't stay still!).

And oh my God, the instructions are endless.

And confusing.

So confusing.

And boring.

"You really used to play this as a kid?!"

He looks up.

"It was great fun!"

Really?!

All I can think is 'no wondered they stopped making it!'

So I suggest we get started and refer to the instructions when needed.

Which was basically all of the time.

And eventually it ends.

And the kids and I breathe a huge sigh of relief, which naturally upsets him as it's ruined his vision so he ends up in the shed.

So not wanting to be the one to bring a halt to 'Family Fun Time' I do my bit and have a hunt around eBay and find 'Monopoly Millionaire' which, from what I can gather uses the principles of the standard game of Monopoly, which he loves, but the first one to a million pound wins.

Win win for all of us.

We can all start the game together and finish the game together and sure enough, it does exactly what it says on the tin.

Or rather... the box.

So we set the game up together, read through the rules and our son suddenly and without warning jumps off his chair, disappears off and returns several minutes later holding some scrap paper, a pen and his scientific calculator.

I half expected him to also be wearing half moon glasses and those metal sleeve holder armband things that accountants wear (stereotypically I mean).

"What's all that for?" my husband asks.

"To keep count of my money!"

"Surely you can just *count* it?"

"No... this way I can always see exactly what I have so I know the exact minute I hit a million!"

Well he won that game three times!

And when I say he won the game *three times* what I actually mean is that he was very good at adding his money up but not so good at remembering to subtracting it.

Plus, this actually made the game last three times as long as after every turn he had to re-calculate his total worth and no one was allowed to take their go until it had been done in case he *had* won.

So if you landed on his property and had to pay out we all had to wait until he'd taken the rent, worked out how to turn the calculator back on again, punched in the sums, written it down on the piece of paper, realised it didn't look right, done a quick stock check, realised he had less money than he had written down, start again from the very beginning of his workings out adding and subtracting what he had written down from the very start of the game, then accuse one of us of stealing some of his money, then realising that he'd been in the room the entire time, then acknowledging that perhaps it's possible he forgot to make a note of the fifty Monopoly dollars he had to pay to get out of prison, write off the incorrect amount, get a new piece of scrap paper and starting again before finally giving his sister the go ahead to take her go.

And if he landed on *your* property then you might as well have gone and made a cup of tea.

And, if you have kids, you'll know that there's nothing worse than having a child think they've achieved something, make a big song and dance about it, and then find out that they're wrong.

And when you add this equation in along with a smug, *doesn't really know anything about how to talk to kids,* husband, you'll know that it's a recipe for disaster.

And sure enough it was.

Resulting in, after our son's third affirmation and subsequent barrage of light-hearted, but not taken that way, Mickey taking from said husband, the game board getting sent flying high into the air, our son storming out and my husband back in the shed.

Again!

But despite all of this *'Family Fun Time!'* continues on.

And with just one major change.

Which admittedly does seem to be helping.

We no longer play our Sunday afternoon board game soirée in the dining room.

No.

We now play it in the shed.

As that's where my husband seems to spend most of his time!

Chapter Twenty Seven

Life Lessons

The husband's entry

I knew it was going to be one of those days!

There I am, minding my own business, trawling through the usual hundred e-mails I have received overnight (all crap) when it suddenly starts.

Thump.

Thump.

Stomp.

Bang.

And then a sound like a cat having its tail slammed in a wardrobe door.

Followed by another similar sound.

So I head upstairs to find out what the bloody hell is going on, as my son's bedroom sits directly above my home office, and I find my son, in nothing but his pants, twirling a pair of football socks around his body resembling Bruce Lee with a pair of nunjacks.

"What the hell are you doing?"

He turned to me and, without even the slightest hint of surprise that I had just been watching....

Or embarrassment for that matter....

Simply announced, in his best Hollywood dramatic voiceover style....

"SOCK NINJA!"

And so there it was...

'*Sock Ninja*' was born.

Now it wouldn't have been so bad.

And may even have been, perhaps, *slightly* amusing.

However, I don't actually recall sending him up to his bedroom, telling him to strip down to his pants and then stand in front of his bedroom window and in full view of the neighbours do his best impression of a demented Jackie Chan.

I do however remember asking him to hurry up and finish his breakfast, put the plate and his empty glass in the sink and then go and put his pyjamas in the wash basket and get his school uniform on.

ASAP!

I don't know if that's the same kind of experience that all parents have with their kids.

You tell them to do one thing and no sooner have they turned their back on you they have *completely* forgotten what it was you just said, or even that you actually just spoke to them at all, and so they wander off getting distracted by the first shiny thing they pass.

Or in my son's case....

The first *thing* he passes -- shiny or not!

Having watched that '*Child Genius*' programme once where overly pushy parents subject their kids to nationwide public ridicule all in the interest of entertaining TV, I can only assume that it's not, as I can't imagine one of those parents instructing their child genius to head upstairs after breakfast and brush their teeth ready to leave for school in ten minutes time and then realising that their offspring hasn't returned and it's now nine minutes later and so therefore they should be at least waiting in the hall with satchel, coat and shoes on so consequently wander upstairs to find out what's going on and on entering their son's bedroom discover their son standing in front of the mirror, his pet lizard balanced precariously on top of his head announcing that he's invented the 'Hat Lizard'.

And Boris, his poor unfortunate pet lizard sitting on top of his bonce looking well and truly pissed off.

And the girl's no more intelligent.

I often thought, as there was clearly no hope for the boy, that I could simply focus all my efforts on the girl, especially as the odds of her being the higher earner are greatly stacked in her favour and so it's more likely that she'll be the one to earn enough money to be able to buy me that Lamborghini I've always wanted... but this all literally *gushes* out of the window five minutes after she gets out of bed.

As any parent will know, from 'rising' to 'out the door' on any school day morning is the most stressful thing you can go through.

More stressful, for example, than meeting your future parents in law for the first time, particularly when your potential future father-in-law is VERY protective over his daughter AND owns his own shotgun, as mine did (and still does).

So breakfast has to be a matter of precision timing to ensure it's ready at the exact moment they are dressed and heading downstairs because any delay at this stage in the operation will result in a massive throwback of time -- much like in that movie 'The Butterfly Effect'.

And all time-travel related movies for that matter.

So, I hear her rising, and the toast goes in, the oil is already heating up in the pan and the eggs are whipped up in the bowl by its side.

Baked beans in the microwave set for one minute.

Yeah, I try to avoid microwaves if ever I can, especially now that we've all moved into the twenty first century, as there's something a little unnerving about nuking your food and then eating it.

However I also try to avoid having too many things to focus on at exactly the same time as well and it's a damn site easier to press 'START' on the microwave than it is to try stirring a pan of baked beans with one hand as well as making the perfect scrambled egg with the other all while keeping a third eye on the toaster because if you don't then it WILL burn the toast (is it *'burn the toast'* or *'burn the bread'*?) all while ensuring I don't ruin anything -- and normally end up ruining *everything*.

"BREAKFAST'S ON THE TABLE!" I shout up.

It's not, but I know that if she thinks it is she'll hurry the hell up.

"OKAY, I'M JUST DOING MY HAIR!"

"IT'S GETTING COLD!" is my standard five minutes later reply as I'm dishing it all up, piping hot.

"YES, I'M DOING MY HAIR!"

"I'M JUST SAYING AS I KNOW YOU DON'T LIKE COLD BAKED BEANS!"

And so this back and forth continues in a similar manner with me bouncing between statement two *'it's getting cold'* and statement five *'I'm just saying etc,...'* and her referring back to statement four *'yes I'm doing my hair'* like some kind of obscure flow chart, until she eventually enters the kitchen some twenty minutes later and I'm expecting to see some incredible hair creation that Vidal Sassoon would have been envious of... and it's just in a ponytail.

And I've given up asking *'is that it?'* now in the same way that she's given up informing me that her beans are cold.

I do think my kids have the magpie gene in them though as it doesn't matter what they are supposed to be doing or heading off to do, if something shiny suddenly catches their eye, then that's it.

It's like their brain goes into etch-a-sketch mode.

My son is learning to play the guitar.

And I say *learning* to play.

He's plinking the strings with a face like a smacked arse under masses of duress.

He basically wants to be Slash from Guns n Roses but without *any* of the effort put in.

So, as we bought him a guitar and also pay for him to have guitar lessons and much like the agreement we had with him when he plagued us for months on end to get Boris and we informed him that if we do he has to continuously look after him, even when he gets bored -- which WILL happen, and him telling us that he'll *never* get bored with a pet lizard and then consequent getting bored within about three weeks of having him and so now I have to look after Boris otherwise if it was left to my son Boris would have kicked the bucket about six weeks after he got him -- and I'm pretty sure my son wouldn't have even noticed, I force him to practice for ten minutes a day.

And of course I have to remind him that its guitar practice time every day because if I don't then he pretends to forget -- every day... and so guitar practice never gets done.

So for your better understanding of:

1. How guitar practice goes each day in our household.

And

2. How my son's mind works.

For arguments sake let's pretend it's six O'clock in the evening.

I'll say something like *'right son, ten minutes on your guitar, off you go'*.

He'll then plod off taking literally a whole minute to get upstairs and into his bedroom where he keeps his guitar.

So let's assume it's now one minute past six.

Then, I give it a further two minutes and, as is always the case, won't have heard the slightest plinking taking place, and knowing that there's no point in shouting up to him, I then head on up to see what the hell he's doing and he'll be sitting on the floor, guitar still in its case and on the floor next to him, flicking through one of his *'learn how to play the guitar like Eric Clapton'* music books.

"What are you doing?"

"Choosing a song!"

So I grab the book off him, flick it open at any random page and hand it back along with the clear and concise instruction… *'this one!'*

And then I walk out of his bedroom and stand just slightly out of view and listen to him, sure enough, start plinking.

So it's now about five minutes past six.

Then he'll appear at my office door a minute later and ask if he can play something for me.

I'll naturally agree as I like to show a little bit of enthusiasm, at which point he'll then head back upstairs to get his guitar.

And bring it back down stairs.

Then find a suitable spot in the office to rest it.

Then head back upstairs to get his music book.

Then return with the book and sit down on the floor next to his guitar.

Then pick up his guitar and position it ready to play.

Then open his book and search for the song he's just been plinking.

Then find it and try to get the book to stand up by resting it on the floor in front of him so he can see it, which of course as it's quite big and flimsy it won't, so I eventually, patience fast running out, suggest that I hold it open at the song for him.

Then twiddle with the tuning things at the end of the guitar but not actually tune it and instead turn each one ninety degrees one way and then ninety degrees back to exactly where it originally was.

Then announce that he's left his plectrum in his room so go to stand up at which point we have the usual thirty second discussion about him using his fingers to strum the strings with and him insisting he can't, and so then heading off to get his plectrum leaving me still holding his music book open like a fool.

Him then reappearing at the doorway some thirty seconds later to announce that when he was in his bedroom he noticed the time and as it's now quarter past six not only are his ten minutes up but he's actually done an extra five minutes today and can he check his e-mail when I'm done on the computer.

And you know when it's just not worth the effort of even discussing it with him!

He bounded in to me once informing me that he needed to search for some ghost sounds that he could play on his guitar.

"Ghost sounds?"

Apparently it was for something he was doing at school and needed to be able to play ghost sounds on his guitar.

Turns out, as usual, it was NOTHING to do with school, as is *always* the case, and just him wanting to play some spooky music with his band mates.

Plus, try punching *'ghost sounds'* into Google and see what it brings up!

It certainly wasn't what he was expecting.

And his *'band mates'*… well, let's just say that they are no 'Queen'.

They are instead the kind of band that has three members, two of which both play the lead guitar… and they're both acoustic, and the third member plays a cheap pair of drums, that might as well be some upturned buckets, which he wasn't meant to play but even they agreed that they couldn't really put a band together that only actually consisted of three lead guitarists and he drew the short straw.

Oh, and all three of them are the lead singer.

And I literally mean, all three of them sing the same words at the same time and in the same harmony.

If you took a typical football crowd and got them to sing one of their standard and usual racist style, fight antagonising chants, then that would probably stand a better chance of getting to number one than anything they write.

And mainly because all the songs they write are about Minecraft.

And I did suggest that his sister join their band as she *can* actually sing a little.

And her *'can actually sing a little'* is a damn sight better than the cats chorus that they churn out, but apparently, other than his mates sister as his mate has no real choice over that one, there are NO girls allowed within a ten mile radius of his mates garage (where they practice) so that rules that out.

I haven't yet had the heart to tell them about 'groupies'.

They put on a show for us once.

It lasted all of three minutes.

In fact it took us longer to drive round to his mate's house.

And you know when you are literally sat on the fence not knowing whether to encourage them….

Or suggest they just set fire to their instruments and be done with it.

Like when you watch the X-Factor and Simon Cowell has just publically ridiculed some poor talentless, tone deaf wannabe on national TV and the wannabe says *well every else says I'm really good* and Simon Cowell says *who's everyone* and it turns out it's actually just their mum.

I don't want my son to be THAT kid!

So as their older and somewhat, wiser father, I try desperately to impart my years of knowledge and experience on to my kids in the form of stories, life lessons and experiences.

You know, to help them get ahead in life.

Get a bit of a jump start.

And so they can avoid many of the pitfalls and obstacles that we, as adults, have ourselves been through.

But of course none of it sinks in.

Pretty much like none of it sunk in when my parents used to try doing the same thing with me.

And so for the most part I'm happy to let them continue on their carefree, childhood journey.

All innocent and naive.

Because I know….

For sure….

That one day, when I hit *old age* the roles will be reversed.

And then I'll be able to get my own back on them!

Chapter Twenty Eight

Money, Money, Money

The husband's entry

I stared down the barrel of a .45 calibre pistol.

The armed robber stood opposite, demanding the money from the cash tin sitting on the counter behind.

Only a small wooded reception desk stood between us.

My only staff member stood frozen by my side -- eyes wide with fear.

I, strangely enough, remained rather calm.

Perhaps a little *too* calm.

"Go screw yourself!" I announced.

Through his stocking mask I could just make out the look of surprise on his face.

Those words, the last ones he expected to hear from little old me.

He pushed the gun closer towards my chest.

"I'm not f$*^%~# about now... HAND OVER THE CASH!"

I shook my head.

"Forgive me, I obviously didn't make myself clear enough. I said... GO SCREW YOURSELF!"

He pulled back the hammer on the Glock he was holding.

It locked into place.

His index finger slowly squeezed the trigger tighter, increasing the pressure on it.

My staff member started to panic but was unable to speak with terror.

Had he have done, I'm sure he would have said something along the lines of *'just give it to him and he'll go. It's not worth dying for'*.

Ever the optimist!

I, however, just like the USA, don't negotiate with terrorists.

Plus I've never, ever, gone down the sensible path.

And today was going to be no different.

I locked horns with my assailant.

The atmosphere was tense -- like in a game of Russian roulette, tense (not that I've ever played Russian roulette, although I did see Derren Brown do it live on TV once and it's *that* kind of tense I'm talking about. If you didn't see the Derren Brown thing yourself then just try to imagine a really tense situation and it was like that).

The robber's eyes narrowed.

So did mine.

Then, suddenly the hammer shot forward on the gun.

There was a sudden flash of gun powder igniting.

Followed instantly by a massive explosion as the bullet powered its way down the barrel.

It was deafening.

I only had time to hear the scream from my staff member as, with little to no regard for his own life, let alone his own safety, he threw himself in front of me, knocking me onto the floor and out of the way.

"NOOOO!"

THUD -- the bullet hit him full force in his chest.

Blood splattered all over the counter.

All over the walls.

And all over me.

His limp body collapsed in a bloody heap onto the floor next to me.

I grabbed his limp and shattered torso.

Cradled it in my arms.

Screamed out at the top of my lungs... "Why? WHY? TAKE ME INSTEAD! TAKE ME!!"

I looked up fearing the worst, but the gun man had already taken to his heels and fled the scene.

The door bounced closed behind him.

And as I stared helpless into my staff member's arms, he spluttered out his last dying words....

"Tell my wife I love her."

And then it all went dark.

Yeah, so I'll admit... none of that actually happened although in my defence, I'm pretty sure when he recounts his side of events later, that's more or less exactly how it played out in my staff members head.

Like a scene from a Bruce Willis movie.

And if you *can* picture that, then you can pretty much picture the kind of person my staff member is.

In my head however....

Well let's just say... it was not quite so dramatic!

You see it was a normal, quiet, Saturday morning not long after we had opened and I was alone in the store with just my staff member for company when the door swung open and in strolled a potential customer.

I greeted him with the usual welcoming smile and we engaged briefly in the standard and customary small talk that so befits this typical situation before the customer made his announcement to me and the real purpose of his visit which wasn't that he longed for adult company and / or conversation and was, of course, to hand over some of his hard earned money in exchange for some of my favoured goods.

I retrieved, with ease I hasten to add, the precise goods that he had come in to acquire and he, in turn, handed over fifteen pounds made up of no less than one ten pound note and one five pound note for an item that was on sale for twelve pounds.

I opened the cash tin resting on the side of my reception counter and took out three pound coins -- his change.

In the simple process of retrieving those three pound coins I did happen to make a mental note that two of the pound coins appeared to be particularly shiny, especially when compared, in that brief moment, to the rather dull looking third one that also made up the gentleman's change.

I decided, however, to make nothing more of it as I started to pour them into his open and eagerly expectant hand.

As we were so quiet, my staff member, using his own initiative, had already bagged up the customer's purchase and was very considerately handing it over to him, thereby also helping to contribute to the overall customer experience this happy chappie was already experiencing through our extremely courteous and helpful ways.

Now this goods for cash exchange moment happened at more or less the exact same time as I proceeded to drop the three pound coins into the open palm of the customer's hand and it is at more or less that exact same moment that my staff member clocked one of the pound coins and shouted....

"WAIT!"

Now I jumped almost as much as the customer but it was simply too late... the coins had already left my hand and were now entering the vicinity of the customer's hand by way of a gravity induced rapid downward movement, when, to add even more excitement to the already over excited staff member, he proceeded to snatch (yes, literally *snatch*) the coins back from the already closing hand of our customer before they were fully in his grasp.

Poor bugger!

And then there was a momentary pause in proceedings while both myself and the customer stared in disbelief at our mutual 'assistant' who himself stood with fist closed tightly around the three pound coins as he stood there with a self satisfied smile slapped right over his weasely little face.

"What? What's wrong"

"You don't want to give *those* away... they're rare they are!"

"What... pound coins?"

"No... *these* pound coins"

He opened his sweaty little palm and the three of us gazed in awe upon it like one might gaze upon the '*one ring*' as it rested in Frodo's tiny little palm.

And I'll admit... to me they just looked like three regular pound coins.

But apparently they were both so much more!

"Yeah, well not that one," my staff member admitted as he picked out the dull, un-shiny one and with some considerable disdain, cast it back into the still outstretched palm of our shocked customer.

'But them two,' he further announced (and yes 'them' as opposed to 'those') as he pointed (in case we couldn't see them) towards the two remaining golden nuggets.

"Rare?"

"Yeah, me mate collects them."

And so it would appear (according to my staff member) that the royal mint makes the occasional batch of one and two pound coins for some special occasions (whatever that may be) and consequently brandishes them with a rather unique picture on the opposite side of the queen's head in order to mark that special occasion and apparently it's these unique ones that are worth more than the normal ones.

As you would naturally expect.

It would also turn out that his 'mate' has a couple of rare two pound coins worth fifty pounds each.

Apparently.

And as always, I find that extremely hard to believe.

So how... exactly, does it work then?

I mean, do you go into your local KFC, order a bargain bucket meal for nine ninety nine, hand over your rare two pound coin and ask for forty pounds and a penny change?

They're going to laugh you right out of there.

But no, apparently, you keep them safe, and in twenty years time, they'll be worth thousands of pounds (again... apparently!), and if I don't believe him then just look on eBay as there's loads of people selling rare pound coins and I can just take a look for myself.

Now, I'm sure this *is* probably the case.

And I'm sure that there may well be some rare one pound and two pound coins floating around in circulation that no one realises are rare but at that moment in time, my staff member had two supposedly rare pound coins in his hand and the customer had one regular pound coin, which in my book actually made the regular pound coin rarer than the rare ones.

So needless to say, and not being one to want to miss out on the slight possibility that I may have a pound coin (or two even, in this case) that is actually worth fifty pounds (or to be honest, I wouldn't even care if they were just worth two pounds each because at least that would be something as it would certainly be double their current face value) so I fished out two pounds worth of extra change which mainly consisted of some silver and lots and lots of copper, much to the protest of the customer, faced the fact that that customer would be taking his business elsewhere in future and consequently returned home with them so that I could have a good look on eBay, begin my rare coin collecting hobby and secure mine and my family's financial future.

"Can I use the computer?" I asked my wife who was just casually surfing through the usual thousand clothing websites -- her standard *'time whiling away'* activity.

"Yes... when I'm finished"

Now we generally have two perspectives that take place in this regular and most common situation we both tend to find ourselves in.

My perspective, which is....

'Everything might change in the five minutes it takes to get you off that bloody computer so I need it right NOW!'

And my wife's perspective, which is....

'Nothing's going to change in the five minutes that follows your repetitive and somewhat consistently boring request to gain access to this computer and if it is that urgent, then just fire up the bloody Ipad and stop mithering me!'

So I drop the big one on her!

"Honey... I have a couple of rare pound coins here and I want to check out exactly how much they're worth."

She glances at them resting in my hand and she too cannot mistake the fact that they are indeed very shiny and so, not wanting to rule out the possibility that it might be like that scene in *'Only Fools and Horses'* where the old wrist watch that they've had sitting in the garage lock up for the past ten years turns out to be worth millions and if they had discovered that sooner they'd not have had to go through all the tough times they had to endure while constantly looking for the perfect *'get rich quick'* scheme (and in turn we, of course, would not have had some of the greatest moments in TV comedy history).

So she budges over.

And by budges over I mean she just slides the office chair a few inches to her right thus *'kind of'* granting me access to the PC but with nothing to actually sit on so she still maintains that air of being in control.

So I kneel down next to her (like some peasant kneeling next to its monarch) in order for me to be able to fully access the keyboard and thus avoid leaning over the office desk (which is positioned much too low -- another long story) and consequently ending up with bloody back ache.

Again!

Thanks honey (and I say that with the relevant sarcasm that it necessitates)!

And I'm sure that the only reason my wife is staying around to watch those next few precious clicks on the mouse is to solidify her belief that I am indeed... a *'gullible fool'*.

It doesn't take long.

So, I punch *'rare one pound coins'* into Google and in turn it throws back hundreds of links with loads of images of what I naturally assume to be some very rare one pound coins.

I glance at my wife and nod towards the screen.

She smiles back at me in acknowledgement but not one of those *'well done you'* smiles but more of a *'just keep going'* smile.

I click on the images link.

Study them all.

Can't find mine.

So I punch in the names of the 'two flowers' that appear on the reverse of the pound coins that now sit on the office desk in front of us both.

Still nothing.

"I don't think that's a snowdrop" my wife announces with that usual *'lack of interest'* tone that she often uses to disguise her *actual* interest and without even bothering to lift the coin off the office desk to double check herself -- highlighting to me the fact that she *is* actually very much interested.

I delete 'snowdrop' and punch in 'bluebell'.

And sure enough BANG, there it is -- 'eBay', my saviour.

I smugly click on the 'eBay' link that Google has now thrown back for me.

Turn to my wife with a big conceited *'told you so'* smile on my face as the link slowly begins to load in front of us both.

And sure enough we're both confronted with my (two) one pound coins ready and available to buy on eBay, and more importantly for the princely sum of....

Ninety nine pence.

NINETY NINE PENCE!

What Muppet, in their right mind, sells a one pound coin, on ebay, for ninety nine bloody pence.

And to make it worse, there's also a one pound and eighty pence delivery charge!

So it's lose lose really.

You either sell your one pound coin on ebay for less money than it's actually worth.

Or you pay an extra one pound and eighty pence for a coin that's only actually worth one pound.

"Finished now?"

That's all my wife says -- *'finished now'*!

So I pick up the two worthless pound coins and skulk off with my tail between my legs, yet again.

And she continues on with her time whiling away activity as if those last few minutes didn't actually happen -- that is, of course, until we have friends round for another dinner party and she has a few too many glasses of Asti Spumante.

And all I can think is that not only have we ensured that that poor, old, innocent customer will most certainly never grace us with his presence again.

But that my bloody staff member will now be promoted to *'Head of Shelf Stacking'* in the back room store cupboard out of the way.

And on a Sunday afternoon for that matter.

When I'm not in!

Chapter Twenty Nine

We Are Sailing

The wife's entry

"Would you like to come sailing with me?!" my husband enthusiastically asked... a huge hopeful smile slapped right over his bright red, sunburnt face.

I really didn't.

I was more than happy here on my sunbed, reading the two month, out of date copy of 'OK' magazine I'd managed to find on the *swap your German holiday books here* shelf in the resort lobby.

Despite its dog eared corners, torn pages and greasy innards from all the suntan lotioned hands that have pawed their way through it over the past few months, it's still like gold dust finding something I can read that isn't written in a foreign language.

To be fair, I do think those swap shop style shelves are a good idea and you *can* sometimes find books that are written in English....

It's just that the only ones that generally *are* written in English turn out to be either 1970's Mills and Boon romance novels or those weird Steven King books that are so bloody thick you'd never finish it even if you spent the rest of your life on holiday.

Plus, the only reason he was asking me to endure a sailing expedition with him was because he was newly qualified.

And let me explain *'newly qualified'* for a moment.

You see, we were on holiday in the Caribbean.

And they're a *lot* more laid back than back home.

In fact they're *so* laid back that his complete and total sailing tuition consisted of him on one of those pointless and tiny catamaran style sailing things with the resident *'couldn't be arsed'* sailing instructor simply pointing to objects in the water and him steering the boat towards them.

And it lasted all of twenty minutes.

Now admittedly I'm no Ellen MacArthur.

But even I know that there's a little bit more to sailing than just that.

"Come on, it'll be really romantic!"

REALLY!

So as he stares down at me with his puppy dog eyes I find myself reluctantly agreeing once again to some mad adventure that he's instigated... like the time he wanted us all to try skiing at some far away snow dome and neglected to tell me that despite this being the height of summer, we still needed to dress like we were heading off to an alpine resort.

So we (he included) stood alongside all the other skiers in their ski coats, salopettes, gloves and ski boots, who had also booked their first trial lesson at the same time as us, and we were wearing shorts, t-shirts and flip flops.

"Is it safe?!"

"Of course it's safe! I've just qualified!"

"Exactly!"

So I clamber on to the boat (sorry... Hobie Cat -- stupid name) along with my husband, and through gritted teeth, do my best to look like I'm going to have fun, as I'm particularly conscious now that most of the beach is watching and I don't want to give the impression that my husband doesn't have a clue what he's doing and this may be the last time they all see me alive, and one of the water sport guys push us out with the gentle reminder *'remember... just thirty minutes, okay?!'*.

Five would have been better.

And instantly we nearly decapitate a water skier bobbing around in front of us as he waits for his turn as my husband is too busy working out which part of the rope he needs to be holding to pay attention to where he's actually going.

"WATCH OUT!" he shouts.

My husband glances up.

"OH SHIT!"

He grabs the rudder.

Drives it to the right.

The boat turns.

The wind hits the sail and whips it violently over to the other side of the boat almost taking my head off in the process.

"Sorry!"

My husband waves apologetically at the water skier who didn't realise how close he was to never water skiing again.

"Right... turn round!" I announce.

"What! No... it's going to be fun!"

"Who for?!"

"Come on, trust me... oh and keep your head down 'cos I don't really know when it's going to do that again."

What was I thinking!

So we manage to get away from the beach area without killing anyone, or flipping it over, and he says *'let's sail along the coastline and have a look at some of the other resorts along the way'*.

"Can we just stay close to *our* coastline?"

"Honey... we're on holiday, it's thirty degrees and we're sailing a boat on the sea... live a little!"

LIVE A LITTLE!

That was the problem.

Right at that very moment I genuinely thought a little was all I had left.

So I kick back a bit and admittedly after about ten minutes and no capsizing I start to relax and even start enjoying it a bit.

Just a bit mind.

But ever the cautious one and, as all my husband needed was Rod Stewart to roll up beside us singing *'we are sailing'* to make him think he was Ben Ainslie, I think I'd better just double check....

"Hadn't we better turn back now?"

"We've only been going ten minutes so we'll just keep going for another five and then that's fifteen minutes to get back. Plenty of time!" he said, with a self assured smile on his face.

Okay I thought... you're the expert!

So we head down the coast for another five minutes and I can't help thinking as I look back, 'we're an awful long way from where we started'.

"Okay, can we turn back now!"

"Honey, just relax... I know what I'm doing."

Fine!

But I wasn't really.

I really wanted us to head back, as our resort now resembled a small dot in the distance and we were no longer passing other resorts and instead were now passing the local beaches where locals were hanging out... most of who were now staring at us.

My husband threw them a nonchalant wave.

No response.

"Okay, I'm serious... turn round!"

"Fine!"

So he moved the rudder attempting to turn the boat one hundred and eighty degrees and it stalled at ninety.

And we sat there -- motionless.

And him still with that smug smile on his face.

I said nothing.

He did nothing.

And so did the boat.

"We're not moving."

"That's okay... it just needs to catch the wind."

We sat there for about forty five seconds, which doesn't seem like much but try sitting still for forty five seconds and then add in a tiny boat, a choppy sea, obvious wind as I could feel it on my body, no movement and murderous looking locals all within swimming distance and tell me it doesn't feel like a LIFETIME.

"Okay... we're not moving!"

"Yeah, he said this might happen."

"Who?"

"The instructor."

"And what did he say to do in this situation?"

"He didn't!"

"And you never thought to ask?! Get me back NOW!"

His smug smile dropped as quickly as the wind.

He pushed the sail across to the other side of the boat using his hand.

It snapped back hard, hitting him full force in the face.

"Bloody Hell!"

The boat rocked worryingly on the waves.

I grabbed hold of the mesh I was laying on.

He then tried furiously turning the boat by thrashing the rudder back like a kind of oar.

It did nothing.

"Get me back now!"

He stopped.

A panicked look on his face.

"What do you want me to do? It's not working!"

"You're the expert!"

He stared at me -- cogs whirring away inside his head.

And then he jumped off the side of the boat.

"What the hell...!"

I glance over to where he'd just resurfaced and watch, in amazement (along with the locals), as he proceeded to swim and at the same time, push the boat around to face the other direction.

And in his defence he manages it.

And so clambers back on the boat.

I just stare at him.

"Right, that did it, now I just need to let some of the sail out so we catch the wind."

So he did.

And we didn't move.

And it was now thirty five minutes later.

He swished the rudder about some more.

Nothing.

He pulled the sail in.

Still nothing.

I took a deep, calming breath....

"Honey, look at me. Focus for a second."

His panic stricken eyes met mine.

"Do you know what you're doing?"

He thought long and hard for a moment and then....

"No."

Great!

"So what did he teach you then, when you went out with him for your lesson."

It would appear not a lot as I now know, and certainly NOT how to sail a boat when the wind is blowing towards you.

He let the sail out.

Pulled it back in.

Swished the rudder about some more.

But for all the movement we managed to make forwards.

Which wasn't a lot.

The tide carried us even further backwards.

"I'll swim back and get help."

"WHAT?" No you won't. Don't you dare leave me!"

"We've been out for forty five minutes now."

"So... maybe they'll come looking for us?!"

And I could see in his eyes that despite the embarrassment....

The shame of having to be rescued.

The disgrace of having to face all those other decent sailors who were probably all now queuing up for their go on this boat and them knowing that he's a complete and utter sailing disaster....

He also wished the same thing.

The true girth of a captain on one of these boats, particularly when you're on holiday, was to be able to effortlessly coast it back in to shore again.

The sun setting behind you.

The sea glimmering all around as you received a hero's welcome, a standing ovation from everyone on the beach, and a salute from the sailing instructor.

And then in the distance I spotted it.

And at about the same time, so did he.

The welcomed red cap of the driver of the resort speedboat as it bounced towards us.

"We're in trouble now!" he muttered.

"I don't care!"

So after a severe telling off (bollocking as my husband puts it) and the inevitable *'what were you thinking? You could have got yourself in real trouble! You were supposed to stay where we can see you at all times'* was over, I find my relaxing, romantic sail taking a slight turn as we're towed back to the resort behind a speedboat travelling at what must be twenty miles an hour, over crashing waves, as the sail slams around so dangerously that we literally have to lay flat on the mesh so as not to be decapitated by it, all while salt water hits us full force in the face to such an extent that we can't see a thing, even through sunglasses, and breathing... well forget it unless you want a mouthful of sea.

And if it wasn't for the fact that we were both wearing life jackets I'm confident we would have suffered even more severe bruising from all the bouncing around we were doing.

And to top it all we *do* receive a standing ovation as we pull into view....

But not from an ecstatic crowd pleased at our return.

Oh no.

From a bunch of really pissed off, sarcastic water skiers who, thanks to my husband, have now all missed their water skiing slot as their boat had to come and rescue us and it's now time for the banana boat.

And so of course now my husband is banned from sailing as he's too much of a liability and their insurance doesn't cover him.

Which, truth be known, should have been a good thing.

Except now he's learning to kite surf.

And you know what?

He can crack on.

Because I know, for certain, that I definitely *can't* be dragged in to that one!

Chapter Thirty

Final Entry

The husband *and* the wife's entry

Well, we hate to say it but it looks like we've come to the end of our little book.

Our little (one sided -- admittedly) conversation.

Our little… 'tête-a-tête'.

Not that that means we've run out of things to tell you about.

Far from it.

In fact, it's a given that with our completely diverse and never ending comical and whimsical family life (please be assured that we are being sarcastic here) we probably have enough material to keep writing until the end of time.

But if we did, of course, we'd never actually get to publish anything which would mean that writing this would have actually been a real waste of time and instead we could have been doing much more fulfilling things with our spare time such as watching EastEnders, learning to jive or sitting in a pub on a Monday evening with depressed old men.

And what's the point in writing a book if no one is actually ever going to read it -- isn't that right Stephen Hawkins?!

So, (cliché alert) we both hope that you have enjoyed reading about the vast adventures we, the (purposefully) unnamed family, have been on as much as we have both very much enjoyed telling you, dear reader, all about them.

And we very much hope you take on board some of the life lessons contained within this *'instructional manual'*.

And for fear of repeating ourselves, yet again, we won't remind you, yet again, that other than changing the names or the odd *tiny* little detail, pretty much everything you just read about did actually happen.

Unless of course you are the kind of reader that instantly turns to the back page of every book to see how it ends.

And if so, I'll save you the trouble of bothering to read any further....

The kids did it!

But regardless of whether you actually bothered to read it or not, *'thank you'* anyway for at least spending your hard earned money on it instead of just buying yourself another pint of beer or EuroMillions lottery ticket.

It will all help fund those court summons we're no doubt going to receive when people finally realise it's them we've been writing about!

And if we do get enough positive feedback, we'll most certainly (*think about) write (*ing) another.

*Delete as appropriate!

So thanks to our two wonderful (no, really they are) kids for giving us such great stories to write about!

And thanks to modern technology for giving some unheard of, not a cat in hell's chance of getting published by a real publishing company, writer(s) a platform and a soap box to preach from!

We hope to catch up with you again real soon.

Now to just sit back and wait for Hollywood to call.

THANK YOU!

Printed in Poland
by Amazon Fulfillment
Poland Sp. z o.o., Wrocław